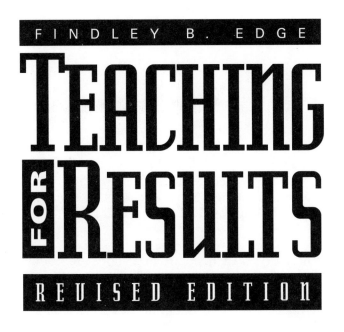

FINDLEY B. EDGE

TEACHING FOR RESULTS

REVISED EDITION

BROADMAN
& HOLMAN
PUBLISHERS

Nashville, Tennessee

4210-94
0-8054-1094-5

Dewey Decimal Classification: 268.6
Subject Heading: Teaching \ Sunday Schools \ Religious Education
Library of Congress Card Catalog Number: 94-21873

Unless otherwise noted, Scripture quotations are from the Holy
Bible, *New International Version,* copyright © 1973, 1978, 1984
by International Bible Society. Scriptures marked (KJV) are from
the King James Version; (NASB), the *New American Standard
Bible,* © the Lockman Foundation, 1960, 1962, 1963, 1968, 1971,
1972, 1973, 1975, 1977, used by permission; and (RSV) the *Revised
Standard Version of the Bible,* copyrighted 1946, 1952, © 1971,
1973.

Interior design by Leslie Joslin
Cover design by Steve Diggs & Friends

Library of Congress Cataloging-in-Publication Data
Edge, Findley B. (Findley Bartow), 1916–
   Teaching for results / Findley B. Edge. — Rev.
     p.   cm.
   Includes bibliographical references.
   ISBN 0-8054-1094-5
   1. Sunday schools. 2. Bible—Study and teaching. I. Title.
BV1534.E34   1995
268'.6—dc20
                                        94-21873
                                            CIP

To my wife,
Louvenia Littleton Edge

Contents

Preface vii

Part I: Introductory Principles

1. Emphasizing Results 3
2. Understanding the Teaching-Learning Process 15
3. Some Dynamics in the Teaching Situation 33

Part II: Teaching with a Conduct Response Aim

4. Making Aims Specific 47
5. Why Aims Must Be Specific 59
6. Securing Purposeful Bible Study 71
7. Developing the Lesson 85
8. Making the Lesson Personal 99
9. Securing Carry-over 115
10. The Teacher Plans the Lesson .131

Part III: Teaching with a Knowledge Aim

11. The Problem of Bible Knowledge 143
12. Improving Bible Knowledge 153
13. An Example of a Knowledge Aim Lesson 165
14. Factors Related to Teaching Knowledge 175

Part IV: Helping the Teacher

15. How to Teach Teachers 185
16. Planning for the Quarter 195
17. The Importance of the Teacher 217
18. Some Theological Aspects of Learning 225

Appendix 233

Preface

The Sunday School has become an important and integral part of church life. It is one of the most powerful forces for good in modern society. In churches of various sizes and types, teachers lead children, young people, and adults in Bible study, seeking together to understand its meaning and significance for Christian living. In spite of their weaknesses and difficulties, God has used the efforts of devoted teachers to accomplish often significant results in the lives of those whom they teach.

Yet most teachers are not getting the results they desire—either in Bible knowledge or in Christian living. There is an amazing lack of Bible knowledge even among those who have attended Sunday School regularly for five or ten years or longer. Although learning Bible knowledge does not guarantee a deeply spiritual life, Bible knowledge certainly contributes to an intelligent faith. Securing results in Christian living is even more important.

One reason why many teachers have not achieved better results is that *their teaching aims are too general and often vague.* Class members have not seen the relevance to their own experience of what is taught. This has reduced the Sunday School classroom to a place to discuss high Christian ideals. Study too often ends only in discussion without sufficient carry-over into daily life in homes, schools, businesses, recreational activities, and other areas of experience.

The objectives Christian teachers seek may be subsumed under three general headings: knowledge, inspiration, and conduct response. A *knowledge aim* is one in which the teacher desires to lead the group in a systematic study of a portion of the Bible leading to an understanding of the meaning of the Bible and/or a mastery of the facts involved. In an *inspiration aim,* the teacher seeks to lead the class in the study and acceptance of a general Christian ideal or attitude. In a *conduct response aim,* the teacher seeks to lead the class to express some Christian ideal or attitude through specific responses in their everyday relationships.

Sunday School teaching is often vague and confused because teachers seek to achieve all three of these objectives in the same lesson. As a result, not even one of the three aims is adequately achieved. The thesis of this book is this: *The teacher will achieve better results by identifying one teaching aim for a given lesson or series of lessons and then working toward that aim with singleness of purpose.*

Thus, one of the teacher's first tasks in lesson preparation is to determine, in light of the lesson or lessons to be taught and in light of the needs of the class, which type of aim he or she desires to achieve. Does he wish to help his class members secure an understanding of the meaning of the Bible and some mastery of the facts involved? Of course, some inspiration may attend this study, and some conduct response may result in the lives of the members. If so, fine. But from the viewpoint of the teacher in this lesson or series of lessons, the dominant purpose is to lead the class to an understanding of meaning and to some mastery of facts. Therefore, everything that is done—the materials selected, the content studied, the methods used—is designed with knowledge as the dominant objective.

Or, does the teacher desire to lead the group to understand and accept a general Christian attitude? If so, inspiration is the primary aim. Or, does she desire a specific conduct response? Obviously, this response will have to be based on a knowledge of the meaning of the Bible and an understanding and acceptance of some general Christian attitudes; but these—knowledge and inspiration—are means, not ends, in this particular lesson. They are instrumental to achieving the conduct response. In this type of lesson, everything that is done will be determined by the conduct response sought.

The principles of this book are not just theory. They have been used with teachers in many churches. The enthusiastic response to these ideas encourages me to believe they may be helpful to others. I have tried to make this book practical by including illustrations and examples of these principles. I have used nontechnical language to be more easily used by the serious Sunday School teacher who is seeking help.

This book may also be useful to pastors, ministers of education, and any others who have responsibility for training in the local church. It could certainly be the basis for study in weekly workers meetings. It may also be resource material for the person who is leading a group of teachers in a study of one of the books in the regular training course. It is designed to be sufficiently comprehensive in scope for use in college and seminary courses dealing with principles of teaching in the Sunday School.

I have undertaken the revision of *Teaching for Results* with the conviction that the book's basic ideals and proposals are still valid. Other ways of teaching also bring about effective learning, but I believe that significant learning is likely to take place when teachers use the methods presented in this book.

In the original edition I gave no indication as to the ages of the class members most appropriate for this approach to teaching. In this revised edition, I limit this approach specifically to teaching adolescents and adults (ages thirteen and up), and only where the teacher has a class in a classroom setting.

The first edition focused almost exclusively on teaching with a conduct response aim. In this revised edition, I have added a major section on teaching with a knowledge aim. During my years of classroom teaching, I concluded my presentation on teaching with a conduct response aim with a brief presentation about teaching with a knowledge aim. I was amazed at the students' positive responses. Similarly, many people in our churches are willing to do serious Bible study. To share this emphasis with the larger public was one of the reasons I was willing to accept the invitation to make this revision.

I have not added a section on teaching with an inspiration aim. I believe this is what most teachers (and preachers) are doing already. Sunday after Sunday they seek to inspire the members in some general Christian ideal or attitude. This is very important. Teachers need to do a better job than they are now doing. But someone else will have to provide that guidance.

Acknowledgments for the Revised Edition

I want to express my deep gratitude to Rollins College and especially to George Grant, librarian, for permitting me to use both the library and a carrel in the library where I could do my writing in the most felicitous surroundings. The entire library staff has been gracious and helpful to me in many ways. It has been a joy to get to know them.

Special thanks also must go to my two sons, Larry and Hoyt. Larry taught me how to use the computer, at least well enough to type. Hoyt, who has taught in the Department of Philosophy and Religion at Rollins College for nearly twenty-five years, though completing a manuscript for publication himself, read the entire manuscript for me and made numerous suggestions that clarified and enriched what I have written.

In the preface of most books authors almost perfunctorily thank their spouses. However, my expression of thanks to Louvenia, my wife, for what she has done to make life easier for me during this period cannot, in any sense, be perfunctory. She is the one who has really "paid the price" while this revision was in process in ways I would not try to describe. She gave herself without reservation. For this I am indebted to her. For this I am grateful to her.

Part I

Introductory Principles

1. Emphasizing Results

2. Understanding the
Teaching-Learning Process

3. Some Dynamics in
the Teaching Situation

▲ ▲ ▲ ▲ ▲ ▲ ▲ ▲ ▲ ▲ ▲

1

Emphasizing Results

Seeking Better Results
  Better Bible Knowledge
  Better Christian Living
Two Dangers Teachers Face
  Verbalization
  Mere Emotional Catharsis
Workers Together with God
Importance of Conversion
  What Happens in Conversion?
  Does Conversion Automatically Produce Character?
The Greatest Task Sunday School Teachers Face

The growth and success of the Sunday School is one of the marvels of our time. Using volunteer lay leadership, with limited time, often with inadequate space and equipment, the Sunday School continues to march forward. Although it has been soundly criticized by some psychologists and educators, the Sunday School continues to enrich lives because our churches are blessed with earnest, sincere, dedicated Christian teachers and officers. Willingly and joyfully they give of their time and energy to this important task.

Seeking Better Results

Yet those who work closest with the Sunday School are the first to admit they are not getting the results they desire. Christian teachers are doing the best they know how, but most are conscious of their urgent need for improvement.

Better Bible Knowledge

In *Building a Standard Sunday School,* Arthur Flake said, "The avowed purpose of the Sunday School is to teach the Bible." This emphasis on Bible teaching has been one of the strengths of evangelical Christianity. Even so, many people who attend Sunday School regularly are woefully ignorant of the Bible.[1]

Knowing biblical facts does not necessarily raise our level of spiritual development, but Christians should know the Bible. Teaching Bible knowledge is not the ultimate aim of the Sunday School, but it is one of its important tasks.

Better Christian Living

Our primary objective in Sunday School teaching is producing Christian living. Even casual observation indicates that we are not seeing lives changed like we should. Too often our teaching dies in the classroom; our goal is to see teaching carry over into life. In the Great Commission, Jesus said, "Therefore go and make disciples of all nations, baptizing them in the name of the Father and of the Son and of the Holy Spirit, and teaching them to obey everything I have commanded you. And surely I am with you always, to the very end of the age" (Matt. 28:19–20). Our task is not just to teach people the content of Jesus' message; our job is

---

1. In a review of studies of Bible knowledge, see chapter 11.

finished only when learners practice His teachings in their daily lives.

Two Dangers Teachers Face

Those who teach for Christian living face two dangers. These dangers are so subtle and their growth is so imperceptible that most teachers are not even aware of them.

Danger #1: Verbalization

Learners may memorize the teacher's words without understanding the concepts. This is commonly called "parroting." Educators call it "verbalizing." This problem of memorizing verbalized concepts confronts all educators, but Christian educators must guard against verbalization more than others because Christianity is basically an experience—an encounter with Christ that must express itself in experience. [You do not truly learn a Christian ideal until you have both experienced it and expressed it in experience. Yet the teacher, in large measure, must communicate this Christian experience to the class by using words.]

Teachers use words to teach religion as learners progress from adolescence through youth into adulthood. Learners memorize verses of Scripture, doctrinal affirmations, and religious vocabulary. That's the problem! Year after year, learners come to Sunday School. [They learn the words that describe religious experiences, and they tend to identify this with having had the experiences.] Jesus pointed out this same problem: the Pharisees verbalized the teachings of the prophets without learning the spirit of those teachings in their own experience. How much this is happening in our Sunday Schools today! Learning words that describe a religious experience is not the same as having the religious experience. [Christianity is a personal encounter with God; it is a relationship, an experience!]

Persons easily become familiar with words that describe religious experiences, but it is much harder to lead them into encounters with God in which they experience the spirit of religion. This is why teachers and learners are satisfied with verbalizing these experiences—repeating words. Of course, teachers must continue using words as perhaps their primary means of teaching religion, but they must also be on guard and take up every weapon to defeat verbalization.

5

Danger #2: Mere Emotional Catharsis

Sunday School teachers also face the danger of leading class members to have only an emotional catharsis. Many people have unconsciously developed the attitude that all they need to do in Sunday School is to attend, sit, and listen. They discuss the ideals of Jesus and how wonderful they are; they discuss the sins of the world and how terrible they are. [But all they do is talk. Rarely do they take any definite action.]

This attitude develops slowly and imperceptibly over a period of years. Young children usually are quite ready to try to carry out the ideals suggested by the teacher. The adolescent is still idealistic and usually willing to do something for Christ. But even during adolescence many of the class sessions just end in talk; class members begin developing the attitude that there is no need to get excited about Sunday School discussion—nothing will be done with it anyway. So the members begin to sit back and just listen. By the time they reach adulthood they have outgrown their childish enthusiasm and their adolescent idealism. They are now more staid and dignified, and they rarely get excited.

What is this process? Older adolescents, youth, and especially adults come to Sunday School week after week, listen to the teacher tell how wonderful the ideals of Christ are and how evil the world is. They agree with what is taught. Their feelings or emotions are touched. They enjoy the lesson. After the session, many in the class may go to the teacher, shake hands, and say, "That was a wonderful lesson this morning. You surely did tell the truth." But when they leave, they do nothing about what was taught. They repeat the same thing the next Sunday, only to come back the third Sunday to listen, agree, enjoy, and have their emotions stirred again. Thus, the process continues, Sunday after Sunday.

There's the problem! People have their emotions stirred so often without making any overt response that they identify this emotional stirring with having a religious experience. [Whether they discuss the need for winning the lost to Christ, or the need for a vigorous worldwide missions program, or helping the homeless in the community, they receive a satisfying experience merely from talking about it.]

This, however, is not a true and complete Christian experience. Emotions play an important and necessary role in religious experience, but experience is complete only when it expresses itself in life and action. An emotional experience that does not lead to response—that is, an emotional experience that ends only in stirring our feelings—is incomplete.

This is unfortunate and even tragic. Christians come to church (this also happens in the preaching service) week after week and have their emotions stirred with no accompanying overt action. [*Eventually Christians desire and are satisfied with only having their emotions stirred.*]

Some say, "I like a preacher (or teacher) who isn't afraid to hit you right where it hurts," or "I don't feel like I have been to church unless the preacher (or teacher) steps on my toes." Still the person doesn't move his or her feet—even though they have been stepped on!

Class members tend merely to come, sit, and listen. Teachers must recognize this and use every available means to keep it from happening. Sunday School teaching should not end in "just talk." Yet ending this problem is not so simple and easy as the teacher might think. People are much more willing to have their emotions stirred as the class discusses some evil in the community than they are to go out and do something to change the evil condition. [*Christian teaching is complete when it results in Christian action—only then.*]

Workers Together with God

How can the ideals of Jesus that we present in the classroom carry over into the lives of our class members? That is our greatest problem! How can we achieve this carryover?

Certainly we must teach in harmony with the way God intended for people to learn. Our God is an orderly God. Insofar as possible, we must come to understand how God has made human personality so that we can teach in cooperation with Him. The Bible is the world's greatest textbook, and the transforming message of Jesus is the world's greatest message. How can we share this experience so that it will accomplish its divine purpose?

Does the fact that the Bible is an inspired Book mean that Bible teaching will accomplish its purpose, regardless of how we teachers do our job? Some teachers apparently think so. They think that because they are teaching the Bible, they do not need to know or follow sound educational principles. They do not want to be bothered with "newfangled" ideas. Their attitude, simply stated, is, "I just teach the Bible and let the chips fall where they may." They even quote the Bible to support their view: "My word shall not return unto me void." These teachers not only need to get the proper interpretation of Isaiah 55:11, but they also need to be reminded of the parable of the sower. In this parable Jesus sought to help us understand that the type of soil upon which the Word of God is sown influences the quantity and quality of the harvest (see Matt. 13:3–9).

Some teachers argue that their indifference to improving their teaching exalts the Bible and emphasizes the power and work of God. Instead, it borders on presuming on God because it seeks to make God do what He is not supposed to do. Satan, following this same attitude, sought to persuade Jesus to presume on God by casting Himself down from the pinnacle of the temple. To do so would have been asking God to use His power in a way it was not supposed to be used. This attitude, despite the sincerity of those who hold it, places the responsibility for ineffective teaching and lack of results upon God. In reality, the responsibility rests squarely on the shoulders of the teacher.

A certain farmer goes forth to sow. From early morning till noon the farmer scatters the grains of corn on grassy pastureland. A friend passing by sees what the farmer is doing. In amazement the friend asks, "What has happened to you? Don't you know you shouldn't be planting corn in a grassy field? You'll never get any corn that way." But the farmer replies, "Oh, yes I will. This is God's seed and God's good earth. He will take care of it." But the friend persists, "To do this is to presume on God. You must plow and plant and fertilize and continue to cultivate." But the farmer again replies, "This is God's seed and God's earth. He will send sunshine and rain. I'm just planting the seed, and I'll leave the results to the Lord." But the friend concludes, "If you don't get a harvest it won't be the Lord's fault. The fault will be with you because you did not meet God's conditions for growing corn."

God created the universe and created the design by which corn grows. This same God created people and created the design by which we learn. The Christian teacher must discover how people learn in order to teach them in harmony with the way God designed them.

Modern farmers are making rapid progress by studying soil erosion, contour plowing, and crop rotation. They learn everything possible about God's earth and how things grow. Farmers now get two bushels of corn where only one used to grow. Why? Because they have discovered how God works and cooperate intelligently with Him. Christian teachers need to study and understand human personality. We must discover how people learn—how God has ordained that people learn—in order to cooperate more intelligently with God. This is how we can expect better results from teaching.

Does this minimize God's work? No, it magnifies God. Does the farmer's study and understanding of the earth make God unnecessary? Not at all. The earth is still the Lord's. The seed is still God's seed. The sun and rain are still God's sun and rain. God still germinates the seed and gives the increase. The farmer just cooperates more intelligently with God and enables God to give a better harvest.

The same is true in teaching the Bible. In trying to understand and follow the way people learn, we do not make God unnecessary. We are still His creation. The Bible is still His Word. God alone can regenerate. God alone gives the increase. Christian teachers must cooperate more intelligently with Him for the great Teacher is the Holy Spirit; human teachers only provide conditions in which and through which the Holy Spirit can work. Doing this requires the teacher to work hard. It takes time to study and gain these insights. It often requires effort to try to apply them.

Consider again the agricultural analogy. Farmers might say they honestly do not enjoy plowing. They would prefer to scatter the seed on grassy, unplowed ground. They may not want to spend money to fertilize. They may not want to take the time to learn new methods of farming. Suppose that one farmer plants the seed and has only a small harvest while his neighbor, following the best in farming methods, has a large increase at harvesttime. The first farmer soon learns. Such farming is not easy, but its rewards justify the hard work.

Today's farmers are paying the price to discover how God causes corn to grow in order to cooperate intelligently with God in growing it. Certainly, as Christian teachers, we must be willing to pay the price to discover how God has ordained that we grow in Christlikeness. We must be willing to cooperate more intelligently with God.

Importance of Conversion

The first half of this book will emphasize the matter of securing results in Christian living through effective living. Because of this emphasis, you might get the impression that I am interested only in results and have not given enough emphasis to the spiritual relationship with God in Christ, the only foundation for action that is thoroughly Christian. I must admit that some Sunday School teachers simply try to get their pupils to "be good" without leading them to understand that truly Christian conduct comes from God's working and living in the individual, not from a desire to "please the teacher" or from any other motivation.

Since it will not be possible to reiterate this emphasis on every page, I want to make explicit here what is implicit as the underlying philosophy in this approach to Christian teaching. [*A personal experience of conversion is the only adequate foundation and the only sufficient motivation for Christian growth.*] In conversion the individual accepts Jesus as Savior and Lord. A conversion experience is not necessarily so dramatic or cataclysmic as the apostle Paul's experience on the road to Damascus. By "conversion" I simply mean an experience in which the individual meets God in Christ, an experience in which he or she accepts Jesus as Savior and surrenders to Him as Lord. Nobody can enter the kingdom of God by virtue of his or her own goodness or by virtue of any process of Christian education. As Shelton Smith has aptly put it, "The Kingdom is God's, and human entrance into it is possible only through divine deliverance."[2]

What Happens in Conversion?

At least five things that grow out of the conversion experience have significance for Christian education.

1. In conversion we receive a new nature. The transforming and revolutionary aspect of the conversion experience has not been sufficiently emphasized in modern Christianity. This experience had tremendous implications in the thinking of Jesus. In speaking with Nicodemus, He said it was so fundamentally life changing that it was like being born again. Indeed, it was a new birth!

The conversion experience is not a superficial or mechanical relationship. Conversion is not a perfunctory acceptance of a religious formula. Paul said, "Therefore if any man be in Christ, he is a new creature: old things are passed away; behold, all things are

---

2. H. Shelton Smith, *Faith and Nurture* (New York: Charles Scribner's Sons, 1946), 125.

become new" (2 Cor. 5:17, KJV). This does not mean that the individual must have a highly emotional experience. It simply means that when an individual gets a new nature something ought to happen in his or her life. The center of life is changed from self to God. New desires, hopes, and ideals are born within him or her. Converted people no longer can say "I'll do as I please," but rather, "I'll do as God teaches." And they say this not primarily on the basis of an obligation imposed on them, but on the basis of a new relationship and new love that has been born within them. This is what they most want to do. On the basis of this new life, doing God's will becomes the deepest desire of their hearts.

2. In conversion we receive a deep desire to know Bible teachings and their implications for the Christian life. We enter the kingdom of God like babies. We may have received previous religious training, but we do not yet know how to apply Jesus' teachings in all the various relationships of our lives.

Through the conversion experience the individual enters a new *way* of life. The person for whom this experience has been deep and genuine should be anxious to study the Scriptures, alone and in groups of like-minded Christians, in order to find out what is involved in this new way of life.

3. In conversion we receive a willingness to follow the Bible's teachings and the Christian way of life wherever it may lead. The desire to know, as worthy as it is, does not go far enough; there must also be a willingness to follow. This is not so simple as it might appear at first glance. It would be relatively easy to live the Christian life today if the only thing meant by "Christian life" is living according to accepted social standards and attending church. Unfortunately, this concept is far more prevalent among church members than we would like to admit. But if Christian living means applying the ideals of Jesus in such a way that they would lead an individual to go beyond the accepted social standards in many relationships and go contrary to accepted social standards in other relationships, then living the Christian life becomes one of the most daring and certainly one of the most difficult tasks in which an individual can engage.

If there is no compelling desire both to know and to follow this new way, then there is reason to question the genuineness of the experience. This is important because, as will be pointed out in a later chapter, this affects the individual's attitude toward studying the Bible and following what is discovered in Bible study.

4. In conversion we receive a power beyond our own, a power that God releases and which, if used, enables us to follow more closely the exacting demands of the Christian life. Many of these demands go against our natural desires and human passions. It is not normal or natural for us to love our enemies, to do good to those who persecute us, or to forgive those who say all manner of evil against us falsely. To retaliate is human. Even to approximate the Christian ideal in these and other areas, we need power from on high.

5. In conversion we receive the only adequate foundation and motivation for Christian living. In the time of Jesus, the Pharisees followed the letter of the Law, but the Spirit of God was far from them. Today it is possible for individuals to follow some of the teachings of Jesus without having an adequate spiritual motivation.

**Five Things that Grow Out
of the Conversion Experience**

1. We receive a new nature.
2. We receive a deep desire to know Bible teachings and their implications for the Christian life.
3. We receive a willingness to follow the Bible's teachings and the Christian way of life wherever it may lead.
4. We receive a power beyond our own, a power that God releases and which, if used, enables us to follow more closely the exacting demands of the Christian life.
5. We receive the only adequate foundation and motivation for Christian living.

Religious teachers (and preachers, for that matter) are always tempted to be satisfied with overt responses that carry the connotation "Christian." [It is much easier to lead people to practice the external forms of religion, or even to make certain responses that might be termed "Christian," than to lead them into continuing encounters with Christ that will cause them to respond, "Not my will, but thine be done."] The Christian standard for life is high; its demands are difficult, often coming into conflict with all our human passions. In these situations—as in all situations that call for decision—the individual's life must be grounded in a firm and genuine relationship with God in Christ. In seeking any kind of conduct response, it is an important part of the teacher's task to seek to insure that class members make their decisions for action on the basis of a spiritual motivation.

Does Conversion Automatically Produce Character?

Will an individual who experiences conversion automatically become Christian in family relations, in race relations, in social relations, in business relations? No. People will become more Christian in certain relationships and activities, but they will not automatically become Christian in all.

Some Christians think that a person who is really saved will immediately know what is right and do it. This is simply not true. The new Christian will know some things that are right, but will not know everything. According to George Gallup Jr. and Jim Castelli,

> The 1950s were ushered in by a wave of post-World War II recovery, with business and industry expanding and a tremendous growth in the cities and suburbs. It was also a decade of religious revival, with rapid growth in church membership, especially in the booming new suburbs. But some social observers have questioned the authenticity of the revival and the depth of religious commitment, charging that many Americans were attending church in greater numbers because it was 'the thing to do.'[3]

Individuals do not necessarily come to have divine wisdom in the conversion experience, nor do they automatically "do what's right" simply because they have been saved.

Peter's attitude toward the Gentiles was not transformed at the moment of his conversion. God brought changes in his attitude later in his Christian development. [Investigations and observations indicate that after the conversion experience, changes take place in a person's life only in those areas in which there is conviction of sin.] Even this does not take place automatically. This conviction must be deep enough to call for the change.

Take, for example, a problem drinker who has a transforming experience with Christ. Because the man was already deeply convicted of the sinfulness of drinking, he will give up that evil habit. But his experience may not affect his business dealings. He may

---

3. George Gallup Jr. and Jim Castelli, *The People's Religion: American Faith in the 90s* (New York: Macmillan, 1989), 8.

continue to extract excessive rent from slum houses. He may see no relation between his rental property and his newly accepted religion. Without conviction of sin in this area, no change will take place. In the conversion experience, it seems that change in an individual's life takes place in those areas in which there is conviction of sin.

One of the tasks of the Sunday School teacher is to lift other areas in the class member's life where he or she is not now living according to the ideals of Jesus to the level of awareness of these shortcomings. In the Sunday School class, members bring their everyday experiences to be placed under the searchlight of the teachings of the Bible. As they consider those experiences and seek the Christian course of action, the Holy Spirit has a chance to convict them of sin and lead to change.

The Greatest Task
Sunday School Teachers Face

The greatest task Sunday School teachers face is this: *to lead individuals in experiences through which they will come to know Jesus as Savior and through which they will increasingly grow in His likeness.* In short, teachers must discover and use the most effective means for securing responses in life that are in harmony with the ideals of Jesus.

In Christian teaching, we emphasize that the religiously educated person is much more than one who knows. He or she is one whose attitudes and systems of value are consistent with the Christian ethic and who, at all times, seeks to translate these attitudes into right conduct.

There is no "royal road to learning." Improvement in the art of teaching and in securing results is a slow and sometimes tedious process. The principles suggested in this book may help teachers improve their teaching, but principles do not apply themselves. If teachers are daring enough to try to use some of these suggestions they may find them hard to apply, at least at first. It is not easy to work out a plan to secure purposeful Bible study or to devise a life situation to make the lesson personal. If you have difficulty, do not get discouraged. Patient practice will make these principles an integral part of lesson planning. After all, we are not seeking an easy way. We are seeking results!

2

Understanding the
Teaching-Learning Process

Five Steps in the Teaching-Learning Process
    Exposure
    Repetition
    Understanding
    Conviction
    Response

From the Classroom to the Real World

Three Misconceptions About Learning
    Listening Is Learning
    Reciting Is Learning
    Memorizing Is Learning

Five Principles of Learning
    Prior Understanding
    Interest
    Need
    Activity
    Identification

What is teaching? When do teachers teach? Christians have spent millions of dollars building churches and Christian education facilities. Rooms have been beautified; equipment has been purchased. Millions are spent to buy educational literature, quarterlies, and lesson helps. Teachers study thousands of hours weekly to prepare their lessons. Thousands of earnest, consecrated Christians volunteer to meet their classes weekly for the avowed purpose of teaching! But do they—do we—understand what teaching is?

Five Steps in the Teaching-Learning Process

Every teacher desires to teach in such a way that what is taught will make a difference in the lives of the class members. How can this be done? What factors make for good teaching? A friend of mine lists five steps in the teaching-learning process: exposure, repetition, understanding, conviction, and response.[1]

Step #1: Exposure

Obviously, a person must be exposed to a Bible truth before he or she can learn it.] This suggests a responsibility for the teacher that is not usually emphasized in a book dealing with principles of teaching. It is the responsibility for reaching people—both absentees and prospects—for Bible study. A church may have the finest and most capable group of teachers that can be had, but their teaching will not help those who are absent on Sunday morning. Someone has said, "You can't teach an absentee." Neither will this teaching be of any value to the host of adolescents, youth, and adults who have never been reached. Just to reach numbers for numbers' sake is a tragedy. But whether we like it or not, we must reach people before we can teach them. Therefore, the first essential in good teaching is to enlist every member and prospect for Bible study.

However, exposure is only the first step in the learning process. Too often teachers have been content with exposing class members to Bible teaching without following through with the other steps in the learning process. What are some of the other steps the teacher must consider?

---

1. Ernest M. Ligon, *A Greater Generation* (New York: Macmillan, 1948), 10–14.

Step #2: Repetition

Public schools have long recognized the need for repetition in effective learning. Parents recognize the same necessity in child training. Children do not learn to practice good manners because their mother tells them one time to do so. How many times parents must remind children to say "thank you" before it becomes a part of their normal conduct! Children do not learn unselfish attitudes because they have been told about them once by their parents. [It is likewise true that developing Christian attitudes and Christian habits is the result of constant, persistent repetition.]

Two practical and difficult problems inherent in the nature of Sunday School teaching as it is carried on today are:

▲ We teach at intervals of one week; people easily forget during the week what they learned on Sunday.

▲ We study different Bible passages each Sunday.

The teacher might well ask, "How can we use repetition in our teaching in light of the fact that we teach only once a week and have a different Bible passage each Sunday?"

These problems are serious but not insurmountable. With regard to the weekly interval, we consider the following suggestion: If the teacher has had a knowledge aim for the lesson, he or she could easily have assignments for the class to work on during the week. Our people need to develop the attitude that serious daily Bible study is a normal and accepted part of their everyday Christian experience. Study during the week would greatly enrich the study on Sunday. The teacher may think, *How can I get them to do this extra study? I can't even get them to study their lesson.* [This means we have not captured our members' interest in the thrilling adventure of Bible study.] It means that what we have been saying in this book is all too true. Our members are content to come, sit, and listen—but to do nothing. It means that teaching must be much more effective in challenging and directing the interests of Christians toward effective Bible study.

But how do we get members to study special assignments during the week? Expect it! Often we get not because we expect not. Class members must come to understand that the teacher means business. Of course, assignments must be in line with the age level and abilities of the members. The members must also be provided with the means for study or with aids in study. People often fail to study the Bible because they do not understand what they study. Books should be available in the church library. Members should be encouraged to purchase inexpensive commentaries to guide them in their study. The teacher should also call for reports in class on these assignments.

The class will not be transformed overnight, but teachers can get some highly desirable results over a period of weeks, even months, by patiently yet persistently leading the class to know that they expect study on outside assignments during the week. In this way the problem of forgetting between Sundays will be greatly diminished. [If the teacher has a conduct response aim in mind, the carry-over, if achieved by the teacher, will lead class members to practice the spiritual truth during the week.] Thus, again, the problem is largely solved.

Having a different lesson each Sunday does not rule out the possibility of using repetition. There are three things that should be said. First, the teacher should learn to use unit aims. In chapter 16 we will discover that, with the conduct response emphasis, the entire unit may have one aim for all of the lessons. Thus, as each lesson is taught, the teacher will be repeating from a different point of view the same spiritual truth the class members should learn. Second, the teacher should make it a practice to have a brief review of the previous Sunday's lesson in every class. In this way, each lesson will be related to the previous lesson. Third, curricula materials repeat biblical doctrines and spiritual ideals year after year to help us at different stages of our personal development. Thus, there is opportunity for repetition.

Step #3: Understanding

Understanding is one of the most important steps in the learning process.*R. R. Osmer says, "At the heart of teaching is an increase in understanding of the subject matter on the part of the student."[2] Yet in the realm of religious teaching, understanding is perhaps one of the most neglected steps. [Many of us learn what the Bible says about various things, but we do not understand what these teachings mean for our daily living.] One of our national leaders once said that all of our national and international problems would be solved if everyone would practice the

---

2. Richard Robert Osmer, *A Teachable Spirit* (Louisville: Westminster/John Knox Press, 1990), 21.

Golden Rule. The statement was received with acclaim; certainly all of us would agree with it. But what would it mean in your personal life if you were to start practicing the Golden Rule? What change would it make in your relationships with your neighbors? What would you start doing for the underprivileged living in your city? How would you practice the Golden Rule in your attitude toward other cultures? You see, understanding what the Golden Rule would mean in specific action for our personal lives is, indeed, difficult.

The Beatitudes present to us an outline for the highest type of Christian life. We believe "Blessed are the poor in spirit for theirs is the kingdom of heaven" (Matt. 5:3), but what does this teaching mean for your personal life? What would you start doing next week that you have not been doing if you were to carry out this teaching of Jesus? I dare say that it would be difficult for you to think of anything. It is important for us to believe these great ideals and teachings of Jesus. But they are of little value to us unless we understand what they mean in terms of specific attitudes and actions for our daily personal lives. [One of the weaknesses of much of present Sunday School teaching is that we teach in vague generalities without leading people to understand specifically what these teachings of Jesus mean for daily activities.

Step #4: Conviction

Understanding is not enough. Conviction must also be present if change is to take place in a person's life. Individuals must believe the teaching to the point they are willing to follow the teaching regardless of the difficulty involved. [They must have conviction so strong that they lead to action] For example, adolescents generally understand that if they followed the ideal of love in their family relations, they would keep their room straight and hang up their clothes. Nonetheless, an adolescent's conviction about practicing love at a given time or in a particular circumstance may be too shallow to result in a clean room. (Ask parents of teens for details!)

Adults have this same problem. [There are many spiritual truths we say we believe, but our convictions are not strong enough to lead us to make our lives conform to these ideals.] We believe that Jesus was right when He said, "If any man will come after me, let him deny himself, and take up his cross, and follow me" (Matt. 16:24, KJV). Yet despite our professed belief in His teaching, our lives indicate that we really believe self-interest is superior to self-sacrifice. Again Jesus says, "Blessed are ye, when men shall revile you, and persecute you, and shall say all manner of evil against you falsely, for my sake. Rejoice, and be exceeding glad: for great is your reward in heaven" (Matt. 5:11–12, KJV). We may believe that, but we do not believe it with such conviction that we as Christians are willing to fight sin with such fury that those who are engaging in evil business and evil activities will revile us and persecute us. We simply do not believe that this is the way to be happy. Again Jesus says, "Bless them that curse you, do good to them that hate you, and pray for them which despitefully use you, and persecute you" (Matt. 6:44). We believe that this is the right way to live, the way for a person to be happy. Yet we do not believe it with the conviction necessary for this principle to control us day by day.

In trying to teach for Christian living, in seeking results in the lives of those we teach, conviction is a central and necessary factor. [It is quite evident that it is possible for Christians to believe religious doctrines and spiritual ideals and yet not have a conviction that is deep enough to lead them to follow these truths in their daily experience.] Thus teachers are made increasingly aware of the difficulty of their task. It is not sufficient for teachers to expose the class to Christian ideals by telling them what the Bible says; it is not sufficient for them to keep repeating these truths Sunday after Sunday; it is not even sufficient for them to lead class members to understand what these spiritual truths mean for their personal lives. Teachers must do all of these, but they must do more. [Teachers must lead their groups to accept and believe those spiritual ideals with a conviction so deep they will become active and directive forces in changing each individual's life in harmony with the ideals.]

Step #5: Response

Teachers must discuss with class members during the session the ways and possible opportunities they will have to express in action the truth they studied. For example, if the lesson is about helping those in need, what should the class do about it? Is there an underprivileged family in the community that the class could help? Does a minority group need assistance? Shall the class go to minister at the county jail? In other words, will class members just talk about those in need or will they do something about helping them? [Planning for this expression of the Christian ideal is just as much a part of teaching as any other phase of the lesson.] In fact, this is the climax and key of all good teaching.

Sunday School teachers recognize that their members have not learned the teachings of Jesus until they put these teachings into everyday practice. Teachers have not taught until their class members have begun to live according to what they have learned. A friend shared this illustration of this type of teaching and learning.

> The boy had a Saturday morning job of taking the week's accumulation of papers from the cellar and burning them. One morning a neighbor boy kicked them all down as fast as he could pile them up. The father says that his own succinct recommendation to his son was, "Sock him!" His son's astounding reply was, "Dad, I don't think that is the way to do it." Knowing from the frequent battles between the boys that this was not motivated by fear, the father decided to find out what was the way to do it. His son finally solved the problem this way. He remembered that the other boy also had a Saturday morning job. He said to him, "If you'll help me do my job, I'll help you do your job." The father finished his report by saying, "I've gone to church all my life, but for practical religion, I'll have to take off my hat to my son."[3]

This is the kind of learning that we seek. This is Christianity in action. And it answers our question: What is teaching?

Five Steps in the Teaching-Learning Process

    1. Exposure
    2. Repetition
    3. Understanding
    4. Conviction
    5. Response

From the Classroom to the Real World

At each stage of life, learning goes on normally and naturally. The baby learns to eat with a spoon. The young child learns to tie shoelaces. The child learns to skate, to play baseball, and to bake a cake. The youth learns to drive a car. The adult learns a voca-

---

3. Ligon, *A Greater Generation*, 15.

tion. On and on through life, learning takes place naturally in everyday experiences.

But this type of learning, while effective, is often haphazard, inadequate, and sometimes inaccurate. To offset these shortcomings, society has established public schools, and churches have established Sunday Schools. Schools go beyond haphazard or chance learning experiences (and seek to avoid unpleasant or undesirable learning experiences) by introducing the element of control into the experience of the learners to direct their learning activities. The classroom situation structures learning with books to be studied, with a curriculum to be followed, and with stated objectives to be sought.

It is exactly at this point we begin to have our problem with helping others to learn. We take learning out of the normal experiences of living and place it in an unnatural environment—a classroom. In the classroom we go about teaching and learning in an altogether different way than we do in ordinary life experience. We substitute authority for freedom; we substitute discipline for interest; we give assignments rather than meeting needs; we study lessons rather studying life; and finally, we substitute things to be learned for living itself.

Yet for religious education, we must place learning in the classroom, for we cannot depend entirely upon the haphazard experiences of life for the complete religious education of children or adults. [Therefore the teacher must seek to bridge the learner's gap between the unnatural classroom situation and the normal experiences of life.] The teacher must seek to identify principles that operate when people learn in the normal experiences of life and use these principles in the classroom. What are some of these principles? Later in this chapter we will identify five of them.

There are, of course, many types of learning. There is a theory of learning for each type. In discussing how people learn we have to ask, "What kind of learning do we mean?" In this discussion, we have in mind the learning that results in changed attitudes and conduct.

Three Misconceptions About Learning

Misconception #1: Listening Is Learning

First, just as telling is not necessarily teaching, so listening is not necessarily learning.] There is a great deal of listening that goes on in our Sunday Schools as the lessons are being taught, but the teacher would be embarrassed if, at the end of the quarter, a simple test were given to find out how much or how little learning actually took place. Listening is an aspect of learning. But the teacher is mistaken to assume that, just because she or he is talking and the members are listening, learning is necessarily taking place.

Misconception #2: Reciting Is Learning

Similarly, reciting is not necessarily learning. Often the teacher thinks the class member has learned if he or she is able to answer correctly the teacher's questions. However, such reciting does not necessarily mean that the member will use that which was just recited in life experiences. Sunday School members at a very early age learn what the teacher expects them to say, and very dutifully they answer the questions as the teacher wants them answered. In too many instances class members do not tell what they are really thinking. Sometimes they recite answers they don't even understand. A psychology professor told of asking a student to define a certain psychological term. The student gave the definition perfectly. Then the professor asked the student to explain what the definition meant. The student replied, "Professor, I don't have the slightest idea." While it is true that asking and answering questions are helpful, mere reciting—mere verbalizing—does not necessarily mean learning.

Misconception #3: Memorizing Is Learning

In the same manner, memorizing does not necessarily mean learning occurs. Learning Bible verses is important for the life of every individual. However, these Bible verses must become directing and controlling influences in the life and experience of the individual. The teacher may be proud when little Johnny quotes in class, "Be ye kind one to another." But if, after Sunday School, Johnny goes out in front of the church and pulls his sister's hair until she cries, that verse of Scripture has not yet become a controlling and directing influence in little Johnny's life. While memorizing Scripture is helpful, the teacher must recognize that merely memorizing is not enough. The Scripture that is learned must be learned in relationship to the present ongoing experience of the individual.

Three Misconceptions About Learning
1. Listening Is Learning.
2. Reciting Is Learning.
3. Memorizing Is Learning.

Five Principles of Learning

Now we will examine five significant principles of learning. Applying these principles in the classroom will help us teach for results.

Principle #1: Prior Understanding

Learning starts where the pupil is. This may seem trite, yet it needs to be stated. A learned scholar may give a brilliant lecture on atomic energy, explaining about the workings of electrons and neutrons. But I will be sitting there restless and uninterested because I do not know anything about such matters. If nuclear scientists want to reach me, if they want to help me learn, they must start on a much lower level of explanation. The things I need to know may seem very elementary to the learned scholars, but if they want to carry me on this intellectual journey, they must start where I am.

Just so teaching Sunday School, many a class member is left behind as teachers progress on a spiritual journey because the teacher did not start where the pupil was. [If the aim of the teacher is to teach Bible knowledge, she must know what knowledge the members already have and what they do not have. If the teacher's aim is to lead class members to deepen in specific ways their current practice of Christian devotion, she must know their present attitude toward prayer, the problems they face in having faith in the power of prayer, and the problems they are having in the practice of prayer.] She cannot teach a general lesson on prayer and assume it will do the members "good." It certainly will not do them the good it would have if she had known their particular problems so that she could have started where they were.

Teachers often take too much for granted. They assume that class members know and understand far more about the Bible and the Christian life than they actually do. Probably the only difference between adolescents and adults at this point is that adults have learned to sit quietly while they are disinterested; adolescents have not. They both fail to learn when the teacher does not approach them on the level of their understanding and in light of their past experiences.

The things the members need to know and the experiences they need to have may seem elementary to the teacher who has studied and understood these matters for a long time, but the lesson will be meaningless unless the teacher begins where the members are.

The teacher must know class members intimately enough to know their level of understanding and their present attitudes in the area being studied. The teacher must begin with them in light of and in terms of their present understanding and development. Learning starts where the learner is. Our first principle of learning is this: *We learn by adding to what we already understand.*

Principle #2: Interest

Learning is based on interest. [In normal life experiences we learn best that in which we are interested.] Which would a fifteen-year-old boy learn best: to drive a car or to wash dishes? Certainly, he would learn to drive a car. Why? He is far more interested in learning to drive a car. When we analyze this rather simple illustration more closely, the factor of interest becomes even more significant. In spite of the groans that accompany the chores of dish washing, learning to drive an automobile is far more difficult than learning to wash dishes. It demands far more concentration. It puts a great deal more pressure on the learner. There is much more likelihood of failure in learning to parallel park. But the fifteen-year-old boy gives himself with vigor to the task of learning to drive. Why?

His desire to drive is so strong it makes him willing to pay whatever price is necessary for success. Are adolescents (or adults) afraid of hard work? Not necessarily. [They will work hard at difficult tasks if their interest is strong enough to make the work worthwhile.

What does this say to those who teach Sunday School? If this is the way God has made us, if this is the way we learn, then we must recognize and observe this principle in our teaching. It means that the question, "How can I arouse the interest of my class in this study?" is just as important as the question, "What am I going to teach them in this study?" Unfortunately, many of our teachers have been concerned only with the second question. They have spent long hours in study preparing what to teach, but they have given little or no consideration to the task of arousing the curiosity and stimulating the interest of the group in that particular study. Of course, what we teach is basic and fundamental; we must teach them the truth of God's Word. But often we merely expose people to the Bible truth, and the exposure does not take. Will our class members actually learn what we teach? That is determined, at least in part, by how interested they are in the study.

Someone may object and say, "These people ought to be interested in what we are teaching. We are teaching the Bible, God's eternal truth." Certainly, we will all agree that people ought to be interested in studying the Bible. But to talk about what people ought to do and what they ought to be will not solve our problem. We must take people as they are. If this then is the way people are, the teacher will ignore the principle of interest to the detriment of both himself or herself and the class members.

A further word should be added: the teacher must recognize that there is a difference between the teacher's interest and the members' interest. The teacher may be intensely interested in the subject being studied, but the members may sit passively and learn nothing. The teacher must not assume that because she is interested, the class members will likewise be interested.

Since learning is based upon interest, the teacher, in preparing the lesson, must make careful plans for arousing the curiosity and stimulating the interest of the class at the beginning of the lesson, realizing that there is little need to continue with the lesson until such interest has been secured because interest is based on need. In doing this the teacher is applying our second principle of learning: *We learn what interests us.*

Principle #3: Need

Learning is based on need. The learner's felt need is closely related to his interest. Again, if we observe people in their normal everyday relationships we will find that they learn what they need to know. Let us imagine that a husband and his wife have just brought a newborn baby home from the hospital, and the wife is confined to her bed. No one else is there to assist. Which will the husband learn more readily, to fix the baby's formula or to conjugate a verb? Of course, he will learn to fix the baby's formula. Why? Because he senses the need.

This means that the teacher must know intimately the members of his class and their needs.] With their needs in mind, he must structure his approach to the lesson to meet their felt needs and help them solve their problems. The teacher may say, "That is not easy to do." Of course it is not. Teaching is not easy. Nevertheless, this principle must be followed if effective learning is to take place. [Teachers must prepare their lessons with this question foremost in their minds: "What need or needs do my members have that are met by this lesson? How can I arrange the discussion and consideration of these materials in such a way that these needs will be met?"

If the teacher is presenting a passage from the Book of Amos to a group of adolescents or adults, she must find in the passage that which the members need in their lives today. Class members are not much interested in what Amos said or did over 2,500 years ago. Because they live in today's world, they have questions that need answering, certain problems that need solving, certain attitudes that need changing.

As the teacher prepares the lesson, she carefully studies Amos but also she observes the lives of her class members. Sooner or later she finds that the questions Amos sought to answer, the attitudes he sought to change, and the problems he sought to solve are similar to those people face today. The teacher must identify the needs of class members. She will start with their needs and let Amos help meet those needs. In this way the class session and the Bible will become more alive for the members. This is the way the Bible should be used: not simply as a source for passages from which devotional talks are made, but as God's guide for life, helping to answer our questions, to solve our problems, and to serve as the backdrop against which our attitudes are to be analyzed, evaluated, and changed when they do not conform to God's teachings.

The primary task of a teacher is not to present material, but rather to meet the needs of the members. [In preparing the lesson, the teacher should identify specifically the needs of the class members that may be met by that particular lesson.] The materials should then be arranged and the lesson taught in such a way that

27

those needs will be met. Interest is based on need. Thus the third principle of learning is the principle of need: *We learn what we need to learn.*

Principle #4: Activity

Learning takes place through activity. [One educator has defined teaching as leading the class members to engage in desirable, purposeful activities.] We all have heard of the boredom that students sometimes experience in school, listening to a dry professor deliver an even drier lecture. Some wit has said that a college lecture is that process by which the notes of the professor get to the notebook of the student without going through the mind of either. However, let us picture students listening to a professor's lecture. They are taking notes. Are they learning? If not, why not? If so, why? If they are learning, what must be present? It is entirely possible for one to listen to a lecture in school or in Sunday School without learning anything.*Activity or response on the part of the student is a crucial part of learning.*

Someone may immediately raise the question, "What do you mean by 'activity'? Do you mean that my adult class will have to get up and act out the parable of the good Samaritan before they will learn?" Of course not. This activity or response may be mental, emotional, or physical. The teacher may stimulate the class to think. Questions may pass back and forth between the teacher and the members. Often, it will be the members who will ask the questions. There may be discussion among the members themselves. This mental activity may lead to learning. Learners may have an emotional response because their feelings are touched, their ideals heightened, their convictions deepened, or their attitudes changed. In any case, when the teacher acts, the member must react for learning to take place.

When we teach adolescents and adults, we are confronted with a problem. As we look at the way they learn in their everyday lives, we become aware they also learn through physical activity. The youth learns to make and operate a radio. The adult learns how to make an effective visit to a prospective client. We call this *learning through experience.* Is this avenue of learning closed to us in our Sunday School teaching? Certainly not. We need to become more keenly aware that activity is not limited to the classroom on Sunday.

Far more often than we are now doing, we need to lead our members in purposeful activities and ministries that find their expression outside the classroom. Indeed, the teacher will find that in carrying out these activities and ministries the members of the class often will learn more practical religion for their personal lives and develop more Christian attitudes than they ever could simply by listening to a teacher—any teacher—in a class session. If the teacher desires for the class to develop a real missionary spirit, then lead it to engage in some missionary ministry in the community. If the teacher would have the class develop a concern for the needy and underprivileged, lead it in a specific ministry in which the members render help to those in need.

However, for such experiences to be of maximum benefit each individual must participate in the ministry personally, not just by proxy. We miss something very real in our Christian lives when we simply give money and let others have the personal experience of helping those in need. Does the teacher desire to arouse within the group a deep concern because of sin in the community? Then lead the class in a ministry to eliminate some flagrant sin in the community—not just talk about it in class. Surely this demands time; it demands work; and the class may get its collective hands dirty in the process. But this is the way we develop the spirit of Jesus and follow His example. Would the teacher have the class develop a consciousness about the social ills in the community? Then lead the group to correct one of these social ills. It will be difficult. They may be criticized, but so was Jesus. We cannot learn Christianity just through talk. We learn through experience. In Sunday School we have a lot of talk; what we need is more action.

This is the way Jesus taught. After a period of instruction, He sent out the twelve and then the seventy both to render service and also learn through experience the joy of service. They came back thrilled with their experiences. We can do no better than follow the example of Jesus in this way of teaching. To do less is to fail by that much.

The teacher, in preparing the lesson, must make plans to stimulate class members in purposeful activity. This activity may be mental, emotional, or physical. It may take place both in and outside the class session. We learn best through experience; therefore, whenever possible lead the class in desirable Christian experiences. Remember that our fourth principle of learning is the principle of activity: *We learn through activity.*

Principle #5: Identification

We learn through identification. Educators have not sufficiently appreciated or emphasized this in the past. Seemingly, they have been so concerned with educational techniques and psychological manipulations that they have failed to recognize the importance of the life and personality of the teacher in the teaching-learning process. Some call this *incarnational teaching*.

> Incarnational teaching is teaching that expects God's revelation in the world, teaching that respects the preciousness of life wherever it is found. . . . It can be expected in the teacher-student relationship, in the qualities of life of every person in the educational process, in the lives of those excluded or marginalized by the educational process, in the joys or tragedies of the moment, and in acts of compassion and acts of anger toward injustice.[4]

This topic is so important that chapters 3 and 17 will deal with it in more depth. It will be dealt with only briefly here.

Ross Snyder, former professor at the University of Chicago Divinity School, once said that, if you want to find out what kind of a person someone is, ask about the kind of parents and other people that person associated with in his or her earliest formative years. This is simply another way of saying that we learn the basic issues of life through personal identification.

We get many of our ideals, our likes and dislikes, our concepts of right and wrong, our attitudes toward minority groups, and many other basic concepts from the person or persons with whom we identify. This is of particular significance for Christian teachers because of our concern to help others develop the fundamental attitudes that will direct and control their lives. In the final analysis, the Sunday School is only as good as the teachers it has for personal identification.

This makes teaching Sunday School easier, but it also makes it harder! Personal identification makes it easier to teach Sunday School because the teacher does not necessarily need to be a master of educational theory and teaching techniques. Yet personal identification makes Sunday School teaching harder because the teacher must live a life that is both worthy of imitation and that inspires imitation.

---

4. Mary Elizabeth Mullino Moore, *Teaching from the Heart* (Minneapolis: Fortress Press, 1991), 92.

Five Principles of Learning

1. The Principle of Prior Understanding: We learn by adding to what we already understand.
2. The Principle of Interest: We learn what interests us.
3. The Principle of Need: We learn what we need to learn.
4. The Principle of Activity: We learn through activity.
5. The Principle of Identification: We learn through identification.

Why does someone identify with one person but not another? Why does she accept and follow the attitudes and ideals of this person and not that person? She tends to identify with people who are most attractive to her, and she will learn more from those attractive people than from others. This involves much more than mere physical attractiveness. It refers to that type of person who embodies in an attractive and appealing manner those qualities and ideals which the individual considers desirable and toward which she is striving.

How does this apply to teaching religion? Unfortunately some teachers live good Christian lives but in such a way that no one wants to be like them. Perhaps equally unfortunate is the fact that in certain instances those whose lives are most attractive are the ones who have little or no religion. The reason for this is not primarily that the latter engage in sinful pleasures that appeal to the human nature of us all. The real reason is found in the spirit of the person's life. The attractive person's life is warm and inviting. The Christian life ought to be more attractive than any other type of life. Whether or not it is depends on the one who is living it.

The Christian teacher should try to embody the ideals of Christ in such an attractive and winsome way that her or his life will both be worthy of imitation and inspire imitation. This is our fifth principle of learning: *We learn through identification.*

3

Some Dynamics in
the Teaching Situation

Factors that Depend on the Teacher
> The Teacher's Attitude Toward the Learner
> The Teacher's Attitude Toward the Material
> The Teacher's Attitude Toward Teaching
> The Teacher's Personality

Factors that Depend on the Learner
> The Learner's Concept of Self
> The Learner's Self-Other Concept
> The Learner's Self-Teacher Concept
> The Learner's Self-Situation Concept

Factors that Depend on the Learning Situation
> Class Spirit
> Classroom
> Class Size

The Holy Spirit as Teacher

Teaching is more than techniques and methods. It is not merely a matter of pushing the right button to get the right response. There are dynamic factors in the teaching-learning situation that go beyond techniques and methods. *Dynamics of teaching might be defined as those factors or forces within the teaching-learning situation that cause action, reaction, or interaction.* This action, reaction, or interaction may take place within the individual, between the individual and the content, between the individual and the teacher, or between the individual and the group.

A twelve-year-old boy has been promoted to a new class. His new teacher has a mustache. The boy has an unconscious aversion toward men who wear a mustache. This aversion will influence the teaching-learning situation. These dynamics may sometimes cause undesirable reactions, or they may cause desirable reactions. For example, a class of girls with the most attractive young woman in the church as its teacher may react toward the teacher with such positive enthusiasm that their mind-set for learning will be greatly enhanced.

These dynamic factors in the teaching-learning situation are often difficult to identify. They are also difficult to control. The teacher must be aware of them and seek to control and direct them if he is to prompt the most favorable learning situation. Anything related to the teaching situation, regardless of how trivial, may be a dynamic factor—what type of dress the teacher wears, what happened at home before the learner came to Sunday School, whether the floor is dirty, whether the teacher had a good night's sleep, and so on. Whatever causes action or reaction within or between teacher and learner affects learning. The following discussion will help the teacher identify some of these factors.

Factors that Depend on the Teacher

The two examples given above illustrate factors that have their source in the teacher. Most of these factors will find their source here. What are some others?

The Teacher's Attitude Toward the Learner

The teacher's attitude toward the learner is important. Does the teacher respect the learner as a person? Does the teacher show a personal interest in the learner? Does his or her manner and way of teaching indicate more interest in the content to be taught than in the person being taught? Does the teacher view the pupils as merely empty jars to be filled? Class members quickly sense the teacher's attitude toward them and react to it positively or negatively as the case may be.

Has the teacher built a close personal relationship with the class? This friendly relationship is often built up through contacts between the teacher and members outside of class sessions, through visitation in homes, through social occasions, through personal conferences, through incidental contacts, and in many other ways. Do class members feel that the teacher understands and fully appreciates their problems, their doubts, their difficulties? The teacher who has developed this personal relationship has taken a long step toward creating a favorable learning situation.

The Teacher's Attitude Toward the Material

The teacher's attitude toward the material to be studied is also significant. If the teacher approaches the lesson in a listless, halting fashion and presents it as though it were dull, dry material that must be covered, the class members will respond in kind. What is taught must be vital and living in the experience of the teacher if it is to create a favorable reaction within the learner. When the teacher tries to teach about forgiveness, about faith, about love for the lost, that truth must be a genuine, integral part of his or her experience. Some teaching leaves the class cold because it comes from an experiential refrigerator.

Christians in the first century knew little or nothing about psychology or educational principles, but they had an exceedingly effective way of teaching—they taught the burning reality of their experiences. When they talked about being courageous in the face of difficulty or forsaking all to follow Christ, they knew what they were talking about; and the learners were aware that the teacher had experienced it. This is one of the fundamental dynamics of the teaching process.

The Teacher's Attitude Toward Teaching

A teacher's rigid and authoritarian manner may create a barrier in the classroom that makes it harder for students to learn. The teacher may have an excellent mastery of the area being studied and may have planned the lesson with care. But if the learners react unfavorably to the teaching techniques, the learning outcome will inevitably be hindered.

Does the teacher have a know-it-all attitude? This often evokes a negative reaction. A teacher should seek to master the material, but learners do not expect the teacher to know everything. The good teacher sometimes has to say, "I don't know. Let's find out." The teacher must be willing to admit limitations without parading them.

Does the teacher seek and appreciate the ideas and experiences of class members? Is the teacher tolerant of the ideas of others? Is the teacher willing for class members to disagree among themselves and with him or her without feeling threatened or insecure because of it? One student remarked, "The teacher hasn't acted the same toward me since I disagreed with her on the Christian solution to the moral problem we discussed last month." This teacher's perceived reaction has created an unfavorable learning situation.

The Teacher's Personality

When one personality comes in contact with another personality, they inevitably react upon one another in some way, either favorably or unfavorably. This interaction between teacher and learner has real significance for learning. The teacher may be a good Christian, a person of high moral character, and a good Bible student with the best teaching techniques; but if his or her personality clashes with any or all of the class members, this will be an important factor in determining whether learning will take place. Probably, it will not.

Four Factors that Depend on the Teacher

1. The Teacher's Attitude Toward the Learner
2. The Teacher's Attitude Toward the Material
3. The Teacher's Attitude Toward Teaching
4. The Teacher's Personality

Whatever goes into making what is generally called a good personality usually contributes to a favorable learning situation.

For example, one is usually attracted to a teacher who has a happy, cheerful disposition and who seeks to make the learning situation a cheerful experience. It is helpful for the teacher to be a relaxed person. Learning usually takes place best in a relaxed, informal situation. The teacher should show self-confidence and inspire self-confidence in the class members. The teacher should also be a person who has deep convictions about the Christian life but who is not overbearing and dictatorial about these convictions. We usually react favorably to those who know what they believe and why they believe it, even though we may disagree with them. However, this must be carefully balanced by a tolerance of other people's convictions as mentioned above. Learners usually are attracted to teachers who are approachable. They need to find in the teacher a person with whom they can talk over their most intimate problems and know that they will find in him or her a sympathetic and understanding friend. There are many other desirable qualities a teacher should have, but these will serve to point out the direction they should take.

Factors that Depend on the Learner

The teacher is not the only one in the teaching-learning situation who causes action, reaction, and interaction. Some of these factors find their source in the learner.

The Learner's Concept of Self

How does the individual view himself? What does he think of himself? What are the central and dominating ideals of his life? What are the goals toward which he is striving? How strong are the drives leading him or her toward these goals? The attitude of the learner toward himself is of real significance when he comes to the learning situation. For example, some young people have high goals in life, but others think no further than next Friday night's date. Those who learn best are those who have a vision of what life is all about and who have worthy goals.

A teacher may say, "I just can't seem to interest Sara in any way." It may be that Sara has never found herself in life. It may be that her listlessness and indifference is due to the fact that she has no goals, no purposes. She is content to drift because her attitude toward herself and life is one of indifference. It is when persons have an adequate view of themselves, a dominating purpose in life, and a drive within themselves sufficient to lead in the direction of that purpose that we have the conditions favorable for effective learning.

The Learner's Self-Other Concept

Another one of the dynamic factors that influences learning is the attitude of the learner toward the group. What has the individual concluded the group thinks of her? Whether her interpretation of what the group thinks is correct is beside the point. The learner reacts to the group on the basis of what she thinks they think. Therefore the question is, "Does the learner feel confident in the group? Does she feel accepted or rejected by the group?" When she thinks those in the group will think well of her if she engages in an activity, she will participate and learn. If, on the other hand, the learner feels rejected by the group, then a barrier has been raised in the learning situation which the teacher can overcome only by understanding the situation and meeting it intelligently.

The individual also learns in and from the group whose approval he seeks. It is, therefore, important what he thinks of the church group in general and of his Sunday School class in particular. Are those who compose his group "his" kind, or does he perceive them to be a group with which he does not identify? It can easily be seen that one's attitude toward the group might play a significant part in determining whether the learning situation will be favorable or unfavorable.

Closely related to this is the influence of group morale on learning. Studies indicate that in developing attitudes and changing conduct the class spirit plays a significant part. Studies also indicate that these attitudes are specific. There was one school that developed a taboo against cheating, but extreme snobishness was condoned by the group. This simply reinforces the thesis of this book. If we are to secure results from our teaching, we must make our aims much more specific in terms of conduct response.

The Learner's Self-Teacher Concept

The significance of the teacher as a dynamic factor in the teaching-learning situation has been discussed previously. Suffice it to say here that the attitude of the learner toward the teacher may be influenced by matters that are important, or it may be influenced by things that are exceedingly trivial. It may be that the learner does not like the way the teacher combs her hair; it may be that she reacts negatively to the teacher's personality. Important or trivial, whatever it is that determines the learner's attitude provides the psychological environment in which learning, whether favorable or unfavorable, must take place. Note that whether or not the learner's impression of or attitude toward the teacher is correct is beside the point; it is still a dynamic factor affecting learning.

The Learner's Self-Situation Concept

This is another one of those hidden forces that influences the teaching and learning situation without being invited, often without even being known. Several aspects of this factor should be identified.

What is the learner's attitude toward learning in general? Does the learner have a genuine desire for self-improvement? This will help determine whether he will study and learn in a specific situation.

Four Factors that Depend on the Learner

1. The Learner's Concept of Self
2. The Learner's Self-Other Concept
3. The Learner's Self-Teacher Concept
4. The Learner's Self-Situation Concept

What is the learner's previous knowledge in the area being studied? Generally the more knowledge a person has in a given area, the more interested he or she is studying in that area. For example, a person who has no knowledge of electronics might be completely bored by a lecture on that subject; another person with a good background in electronics might be thrilled by the same lecture. Some people in our Sunday Schools may show little interest in studying the Bible because our teachers have not yet given them a real foundation of Bible knowledge. (We'll discuss this further in chap. 11.) Lack of knowledge may be one cause of lack of interest.

What is the learner's attitude toward the subject matter? Does the learner feel the material is "old-fashioned and old fogy?" Does he or she feel that the Bible presents things that happened so long ago they have no relationship to life today? Does the learner feel that the Sunday School lesson is only to be talked about or that it is real guidance for life?

Learners who interact with teaching are more open to learning. They feel, "This is real! This is *my* problem!" Chapter 8 will discuss how to make the lesson personal through a life situation or by some other means. Learning takes place best when the learner identifies with the situation being studied.

Factors that Depend on the Learning Situation

Those factors which find their source in either the teacher or the learner are obviously the most important, but we must also consider some factors that inhere in the learning situation itself.

Class Spirit

For want of a better term, we refer to one of these factors as class spirit. The members seem to learn best when there is a strong group spirit and group loyalty among the class members. Does each member of the class have a sense of belonging? Is each member of the class accepted by every other member in the class? Has the class developed a strong feeling of "we-ness"?

Do conflicts among group members hinder the building of a strong class spirit? Conflicts may arise from personal antipathies developed by the members outside of class. They may be caused by social class distinctions or by differences in economic background. Whatever causes differences and distinctions among members will tend to be a barrier to learning.

Is there a willingness on the part of the class to take group action? An individual often is more willing to engage in a difficult activity or project as a member of a group than as an individual.

Does a spirit of freedom and democracy prevail in the class session? Do the members feel free to express their honest opinions or do they fear the censure of others for their point of view? This freedom is not easy to achieve. For example, a class may be trying to determine what is the Christian course of action in an "is-it-wrong-to" situation. Some of the members may come to a conclusion that to them seems to be the higher or more Christian solution and then develop a holier-than-thou attitude toward those who come to a different conclusion. This can be a vicious and divisive influence in any learning group. The freedom to express one's honest views without fear is essential for effective learning in any teaching situation. Otherwise, the members will simply answer the teacher's questions in the way the teacher expects and the others accept.

Is there a corresponding spirit of authority in the class to balance this spirit of freedom? This is important particularly with youth. For a class to have the spirit of freedom and democracy does not mean the teacher abdicates. The teacher must not be so permissive as to be run over by the class. No one respects such a teacher. The teacher is viewed as the leader in the class who not only gives guidance and direction to the learning situation but also gives control. There must be sufficient authority in the class for the group members to understand that their search for spiritual insight and Christian truth is a serious and important undertaking.

Classroom

Physical factors, while not necessarily determinative, are often important influences in the learning situation. Is there proper ventilation? If not, the members may become listless and drowsy, and their capacity for learning may greatly decrease.

Proper equipment is essential for every classroom. As a minimum each class ought to have a chalkboard, a corkboard, and adequate maps. Not only must these be in each classroom, they must be used and used well. There must be comfortable chairs. Some classes like to have a table on which to place their Bibles. A table also serves at times when class members need to take notes if serious learning is to take place.

The arrangement of the chairs in the classroom is also significant. The traditional arrangement with the teacher at the front and the members seated in rows usually leads to a teacher-dominated class. In most instances, the teacher will do most if not all of the talking while the members sit as passive recipients.

Or, the chairs may be arranged in a circle. The teacher takes his or her place in the circle as a responsible member of the group. In this arrangement everyone faces everyone else. No one is in a position of natural dominance in the situation. This arrangement encourages discussion not only between the teacher and the members but also among the members themselves.

Class Size

What is the maximum number that should be in a class? This will vary with different ages and stages of life. In certain groups, there is much discussion today about the relative value of large adult classes and small adult classes. Those who favor the large class emphasize the fellowship that is fostered in the group. The difficulty with this argument is that, while the promotion of fellowship is important, fellowship is not the primary purpose of the Sunday School class; learning is. [Learning takes place best when the learner is given individual attention. There are very sound educational principles which indicate that the small class, even for adults, is better suited for teaching and learning. However, our purpose here is not to discuss the large class versus the small class but to point out some of the dynamics about class size which affect learning.

**Three Factors that
Depend on the Learning Situation**

1. Class Spirit
2. Classroom
3. Class Size

Class size often affects a person's willingness to participate in discussing the lesson. An individual may be exceedingly reluctant to answer a question or express a view in a large class (say of forty or more). It is much easier and less threatening to keep quiet. Some adult teachers complain that they cannot get their members to discuss the lesson. One reason might be that the class is so large the members are afraid or embarrassed to speak out.

For this reason, class size also influences the method of teaching. In a large class, the teacher will almost invariably use the lecture method. There are two reasons for this. First, the teacher cannot get any of the members to say anything, so she just lectures. Second, the teacher realizes that everyone in the class cannot express an opinion. He does not want to waste time trying to answer the questions they might ask; so to save time and cover the most material for the most people, he resorts to the lecture method. Such teaching choices have very real educational significance

42

because, for effective learning to take place, the member must be an active participant and not merely a passive listener.

Members also tend to be lost in a large class. Most large classes have less than 50 percent of their enrollment present on any given Sunday. Those who are present fill the room, and the class president says, "We have a good crowd this morning." The 50 percent who are absent are forgotten and soon become lost so far as the class is concerned. While this is a matter related to administration and perhaps has no place in a discussion of dynamics of learning, nevertheless it needs to be faced.

In those large classes in which the teacher has been able to secure some discussion, it should be noted that often the ones who speak in class are the same ones, Sunday after Sunday. The majority of the class never says a word. Unconsciously, they are lost; they sit on the sidelines while the teacher gives attention to the few who are discussing the lesson. For those who never speak out in a large class, how does the teacher know whether learning has taken place or not? They have been exposed to some teaching, but exposure is not enough.

The Holy Spirit as Teacher

Because we discuss the Holy Spirit as Teacher under the dynamics of learning, do not assume that we identify Him and His work with the psychological actions and interactions of the teaching-learning process. His work is discussed here because it is one of the forces in the teaching situation which goes beyond those matters usually associated with teaching techniques.

It is not the intention here to go into a comprehensive analysis of the biblical teachings of the Holy Spirit as Teacher. Rather, it is our purpose to point out briefly something of His work in the teaching-learning process itself. Two passages in the Gospel of John indicate the teaching function of the Holy Spirit: "These things I have spoken to you, while I am still with you. But the Counselor, the Holy Spirit, whom the Father will send in my name, he will teach you all things, and bring to your remembrance all that I have said to you" (John 14:25–26, RSV). The other passage is even more explicit: "I have yet many things to say to you, but you cannot bear them now. When the Spirit of truth comes, he will guide you into all the truth" (John 16:12–13, RSV). These statements were made to the apostles, but they also apply to all believers (see 1 John 2:20, 27).

Thus, one of the functions of the Holy Spirit is to lead the Christian into an understanding of truth and to give the seeker Christian insight. "What is truth?" Pilate asked Jesus this perplexing question. Today earnest Christians are still plagued with problems involving insights as to truth, particularly as it applies to specific life situations. On every side, the questions are heard: "Is it wrong to do this?" "What is right?" "What is the Christian attitude?" To the true seeker after the truth who will diligently search the Scriptures, who will give careful evaluation to all other available help, the Holy Spirit will provide insight as to truth.

Another function of the Holy Spirit in the teaching-learning situation is to convict. "And when he comes, he will convince the world of sin and of righteousness and of judgment" (John 16:8, RSV). The teacher's basic objective is to awaken class members to an awareness that in certain areas of their lives they are failing to live up to the Christian ideal and to lead them to accept and follow that ideal. Thus the teacher brings to class the problems the members face in their normal life experiences. What is the Christian attitude toward the homeless and how is it to be expressed? What is the Christian attitude toward minority groups and how is it to be expressed? What is the Christian attitude toward the unsaved and how is it to be expressed? What is the Christian attitude in the home and how is it to be expressed? What is the Christian attitude toward society and how is it to be expressed?

Problems such as these are brought before the class for their consideration. In group discussion, as the Scriptures are searched, as teacher and members together share ideas, insights, and experiences, the one not living up to the Christian ideal is convicted of that by the Holy Spirit in and through this process. This is something the human teacher cannot do. The teacher can present ideas; the teacher can share experiences; but the Holy Spirit alone must convict the individual of any sin or shortcoming. What teacher has not felt personal limitations and inadequacy as she comes to the class with a deep yearning to lead class members into some Christian insight, some Christian conviction, some Christian course of action. But after the teacher has done her best, there is a point beyond which she cannot pass. At the point of conviction and decision, the teacher stands helpless before the learner. At this point, the Holy Spirit must take over and do His effective work. The teacher can rest assured in the confidence that the Holy Spirit is always present, always ready, always capable of doing His work.

Part II

Teaching with a
Conduct Response Aim

4. Making Aims Specific

5. Why Aims Must Be Specific

6. Securing Purposeful Bible Study

7. Developing the Lesson

8. Making the Lesson Personal

9. Securing Carry-over

10. The Teacher Plans the Lesson

▲▲▲▲▲▲▲▲▲▲▲

4

Making Aims Specific

What Is an Aim?

Three Qualities of a Good Aim
    Brief Enough to Be Remembered
    Clear Enough to Be Written Down
    Specific Enough to Be Attainable

Three Sets of Aims
    Quarterly Aims
    Unit Aims
    Lesson Aims

Aims and Results

Distinguishing Between the Three Aims
    What Is a Knowledge Aim?
    What Is an Inspiration Aim?
    What Is a Conduct Response Aim?

Learning to Identify Each Type of Aim

If we are to secure results from our teaching, we must know and identify the specific results we desire. In too many instances teachers study their lesson, perhaps carefully, getting a general idea of what it is about. They may even plan a good outline of it. But they teach on Sunday in general terms only. Seemingly, their primary objective is to teach the lesson. Herein lies a major weakness. They have no *specific objective* in mind. If some Sunday morning the Sunday School director should meet three teachers on their way to the worship center and ask them the question, "What was your aim for the lesson this morning?" some would look with amazement. Some would question, "What do you mean?" Many would be seriously embarrassed because they could not respond. Some would give a generalized aim such as, "My aim was to help the members become better Christians," or "My aim was to help them develop Christian character." Few would be able to give a valid statement of a good aim. This is one of the most tragic aspects of our teaching today. Teaching the living Word of God to human beings is far too important to have this kind of aimless teaching.

Aimless teaching has some unfortunate consequences. For example, the teacher tries to cover too much material. With no clear aim or objective in mind, the teacher has no basis upon which to determine what part of the lesson material should be used and what part, of necessity, has to be omitted. By rambling over too much material, the teacher actually accomplishes little.

Having no definite goal in mind as a guide, the teacher wanders down side streets and wastes time on non-essentials, skipping from one topic to another. The teaching will often be unrelated to the personal needs in the lives of members. The teacher, having given insufficient care in preparation to secure a definite aim, merely talks. Class members' problems beg for solution, but they remain untouched and unsolved.

Finally, aimless teaching produces little or no results. It is likely that there will be neither definite changes in attitude nor in conduct because the teacher had no changes in mind.

What Is an Aim?

An aim is a statement of what the teacher hopes to accomplish in a given lesson. Having an aim lifts the teaching process to the level of consciousness, intelligence, and purpose. The teacher may be perplexed about how to work out an aim. What factors should be considered in determining an aim?

1. In determining an aim, the teacher must consider the Scripture passage being studied.

2. In determining an aim, the teacher must consider the problems and decisions the learners face every day. Someone has said that one of the tasks of education is to help people do better what they are going to have to do anyway. Sunday School teachers should seek always to have their aims closely related to life.

3. In determining an aim, the teacher must consider the specific members of the class. Life tells the teacher many things in general, but the teacher is not teaching a group in general but a particular class. Specific needs of class members must determine the teacher's aim. The wise teacher will search the suggested Scripture carefully and find the aim that most closely corresponds to the deepest needs of the class members.

Three Qualities of a Good Aim

From an educational perspective, the teacher can know whether the aim he or she has selected is a good aim. Evaluate it for the following three qualities.

Brief Enough to Be Remembered

When the teacher does state an aim, too many times it is long and involved. The aim states what the teacher wants the class to learn or do. If the statement is so long the teacher is not able to remember it, the class members certainly will forget and thus not be able to do it. Therefore, *a good aim is brief enough to be remembered*, and the teacher should be able to quote it without difficulty.

Clear Enough to Be Written Down

Strange as it may seem, one of the most difficult problems teachers have is writing down the lesson aim. Most teachers think they have their aim clearly in mind. When they try to write it down or state it, however, they find they are confused and usually end up by saying, "Oh, you know what I mean!" Often we think our aim is clear until we try to write it. Then we find it exceedingly difficult to express exactly what we mean. *A good aim is clear enough to be written down.*

Specific Enough to Be Attainable

Our teaching aims have often been too vague and too general. How will we use our thirty or forty minutes next Sunday? As we write down our aim for next Sunday's lesson, we should make our aim specific enough to be attainable within those few minutes. We will discuss this point more fully in the next chapter.

Many teachers ask, "Should I state my aim to the class?" This depends on the type of aim. If you are teaching with a knowledge aim or an inspiration aim, it would be good to state it. But you should not state a conduct response aim at the beginning of the class session. In teaching for conduct response, the aim should become so clear that the class members will be well aware of it. When the session is over, if someone were to ask a member, "What was your teacher's aim this morning?" the member ought to be able to reply without hesitation.

Three Sets of Aims

Sunday School teaching usually has three sets of aims—quarterly aims, unit aims, and lesson aims.

Quarterly Aims

The teacher works with an aim for the series of lessons to be studied in a given quarter. This type of aim is often referred to as a general aim. Since a general aim might also refer to an aim for a year or even for life, it seems that the sake of clarity will be better served by using the more specific term, quarterly aim.

If the teacher is going to secure results from teaching, it will be necessary to have a clear and definite aim for the quarter. This means that the teacher will have to become familiar with all of the lessons in a quarter in order to determine what objectives she desires to reach in the lives of the class members through these lessons. The teacher may say this is too difficult and takes too much time, but it is absolutely necessary if the teacher intends to have unity and purpose result from her teaching efforts.

Too many teachers teach each lesson as a unit in itself, unrelated to the lesson that was taught last Sunday and unrelated to the lesson to be taught next Sunday. If we were to try to picture this kind of teaching, the lessons would look something like this:

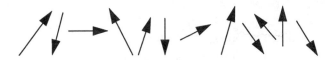

In each of these lessons, the class activity is headed in some direction—but where? With this kind of teaching, the teacher often has little or no sense of achievement or accomplishment at the end of the quarter. The class has covered a series of isolated and unrelated lessons.

The teacher who has an aim for the quarter sees how each lesson helps accomplish the quarterly aim. Each lesson is built on the foundation laid the previous Sunday and leads to next Sunday's lesson. If we were to try to picture this type of teaching, it might look somewhat like this:

Aim for quarter

Actually, this picture will be changed when we consider unit aims. When the teacher has a clear aim for the quarter in mind, each lesson is related to every other lesson and each lesson contributes its part to achieving the quarterly aim. At the end of the quarter, the teacher and class members have a sense of achievement. The point being made here is very simple. The teacher will have a far better chance of achieving results if these aims are known exactly before the quarter begins than if he teaches the lessons as they came, wholly unrelated to any central objective, and merely hopes that some good will come from this teaching. This is so obvious as to need no defense.

It takes time and effort to work out a quarterly aim, but effective teaching requires it. [Teachers must be willing to pay this price or accept responsibility for their ineffectiveness.] God helps those who help themselves, but we have no right to expect God to cover up for our unwillingness to give the time and effort to do a really good job in preparing to teach.

Here is an example of a quarterly aim: "My aim this quarter is to help my members practice three Christian virtues in their daily living: (1) to use the Bible as a guide in making difficult moral decisions, (2) to practice daily communion with God, and (3) to engage in personal Christian witnessing." Having three specific objectives in mind to accomplish, the teacher will be able to make certain lessons contribute to achieving one of these purposes. The teacher who has such a plan in mind at the beginning of the quarter has a much better chance of feeling successful at the end of the quarter.

Unit Aims

A unit aim is one which the teacher has for a group of two or more lessons that naturally go together. One lesson period is all too brief a time in which to accomplish a major objective. Thus, as the teacher studies the lessons for the quarter, he will find there are groups of lessons which are related and which can be used to accomplish the same objective. This objective becomes a unit aim.

In the aim given as an example above, there were three unit aims. The aim for unit one was to lead class members to use the Bible as a guide in making difficult moral choices. Let us say that lessons one, two, three, and four deal with this aim. The aim for unit two was to lead class members to practice daily communion with God. Perhaps lessons five, six, seven, eight, and nine deal with this matter. The aim for unit three was to lead class members to engage in personal Christian witnessing. Lessons ten, eleven, twelve, and thirteen might deal with that subject. If we were to try to diagram the relationship of unit aims to the quarterly aim, it would look as follows:

Aim for quarter

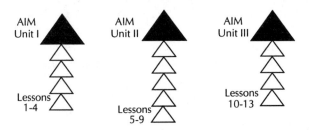

Again, admittedly, working out unit aims may take time and effort, but pays rich dividends in more effective teaching.

Lesson Aims

A lesson aim is one which the teacher works out for each Sunday's lesson. The lesson aim will be discussed more fully in the remainder of this chapter.

Aims and Results

We come now to consider how to determine our aims in order to secure results in Christian living. [One of the major reasons we have not had greater results is that our aims have been too vague and too general.] Therefore, one of the qualities of a good aim is that it should be specific enough to be attainable. The question is, just how specific should an aim be?

The objectives of most Sunday School teachers might be subsumed under three major headings:

▲ To teach knowledge,

▲ To seek inspiration,

▲ To secure conduct response.

Unfortunately most teachers try to accomplish all three of these objectives in each lesson. This is a mistake. These three objectives are not mutually exclusive, but in teaching any given lesson the teacher should have only *one* of them as the dominant aim. If the teacher wants knowledge, then the knowledge aim will be dominant and will serve as the determining factor of what is taught. If

53

he desires conduct response, then this must become the dominant and directing force in the lesson, determining what is taught and how it is taught. *The teacher should establish only one of these three aims for a given lesson and pursue that aim with undivided effort.*

Perhaps one reason we have not had more carry-over from classroom teaching into daily life experience is that most of the teaching has been done on an inspirational basis with some general applications or exhortations made at the close of the lesson. Class members may have enjoyed the lesson; they may have had their emotions stirred; they may have agreed with the generalized concepts that the teacher presented—but they did nothing with what was taught. The teaching was not specific enough, and no definite plans were made in class for this carry-over to take place.

Distinguishing Between the Three Aims

What is meant by a knowledge aim, inspiration aim, or conduct response aim? How do they differ? Only a brief distinction will be given here. (Chaps. 5–9 explain the conduct response aim and chaps. 11–14 explain the knowledge aim.)

What Is a Knowledge Aim?

Teachers who choose a knowledge aim have this as their dominant purpose: *to seek to lead the class in a serious, systematic study of a significant portion of Bible material in order to help class members understand and master that knowledge.* The most significant terms in that statement are the words *understand* and *master.* In the limited time available in a class session, the teacher simply will not have the time necessary to lead class members into a thorough understanding or mastery of the Bible portion being studied. We "see through a glass darkly." But too often the biblical understanding and mastery of many class members is shallow. Thus teaching with a knowledge aim is greatly needed, and we will discuss the knowledge aim more fully in chapter 13. An example of a knowledge aim would be the following: "To lead my class members to master the essential facts in the Genesis account of creation."

What Is an Inspiration Aim?

Teachers who choose an inspiration aim have this as their dominant purpose: *to seek to lead class members to a deeper appreciation of and a commitment to some Christian ideal or attitude.* Of course we already have ideals and attitudes, but we need to clarify and enlarge these from a biblical perspective, and we need to deepen our commitment to them. It is very important for a teacher to understand this aim and to know when and how to use it. Here are two examples of inspiration aims: "To seek to lead my class members to have a deeper appreciation of Jesus as the divine Son of God," or, "To seek to lead my class members to have a deeper social consciousness."

What Is a Conduct Response Aim?

Teachers who choose a conduct response aim have this as their dominant purpose: *to seek to lead class members to begin expressing in a specific way some Christian action in daily life.* This action or response must be observable, and the individual ought to begin practicing the response immediately. This is an example: "To seek to lead my adult class to sponsor a slow-pitch softball program for our young people."

These aims are not mutually exclusive, yet each is distinctive. If the teacher had a knowledge aim for a given series of lessons, she would seek to make the study as inspiring as possible. But the basic aim would be to lead the members to master certain Bible knowledge. The teacher with an inspiration aim would obviously impart some knowledge, but this knowledge would not be a logical, systematic, intensive study of a section of biblical content. In an inspiration aim the teacher might use a very small portion of Bible material or, on the other hand, might use material from many different sections of the Scriptures.

For example, using the inspiration aim given above ("To seek to lead my class members to develop a deeper social consciousness"), the teacher would obviously teach new information; but the primary purpose would not be mastery of a given portion of facts. The exhortation at the close of the lesson might be, "Let's all develop a deeper social consciousness." But there would be no definite plans made in class for the members to give expression to a deeper social consciousness, and no plans to try immediately to eliminate some of the social ills and injustices in their community.

This is not to minimize the importance of the inspiration aim or of developing generalized ideals; we will consider these in chapter 16. The inspiration aim is important because ideals, attitudes, and convictions establish the goals or purposes of our lives, and we learn in harmony with them. If an individual has no deep conviction concerning a given problem, little or no learning will take place in that area. One of the major tasks of Christian teaching is to deepen and extend the goals for a person's life in terms of desirable Christian attitudes.

Perhaps another example would help clarify the distinction between a knowledge aim, an inspiration aim, and a conduct response aim. First, look at the difference in a quarter's aim:

▲ Knowledge aim: To seek to lead class members to learn the significant facts in the life of Jesus in chronological order.

▲ Inspiration aim: To seek to lead class members to have an increasing appreciation of the life and teachings of Jesus.

▲ Conduct response aim: To seek to lead class members to practice three Christian virtues in their daily experience: (1) to use the Bible as a guide in making moral choices, (2) to practice daily communion with God, and (3) to engage in personal Christian witnessing.

Now note the differences as they would be seen in a lesson's aims. Let us say that the lesson for next Sunday is on the first missionary journey of Paul and that the teacher has a class of young people.

▲ Knowledge aim: To seek to lead class members to master the basic facts about the first missionary journey of Paul.

▲ Inspiration aim: To seek to lead class members to be more missionary-minded.

▲ Conduct response aim: To lead class members to engage in a missionary project, such as giving a party for a group of underprivileged children in our city.

The teacher will have a much better chance of securing results in knowledge, inspiration, or conduct response if he has a clearly defined aim in only *one* of these three areas. The teacher's problem arises when he confuses the three and tries to combine them in the same lesson.

Learning to Identify Each Type of Aim

At whatever time during the week the teacher begins preparing the lesson, the very first question to ask is this, "Do I want a knowledge aim, an inspiration aim, or a conduct response aim for this particular lesson?" It may take considerable work and practice for the teacher to be able to distinguish these three types of aims, but learning to do so is a must! The following questions help the teacher learn to identify the different types of aims:

1. Do I want this lesson to have a knowledge aim? Is my primary purpose to teach facts, to give information, or to interpret meaning?

2. Do I want this lesson to have an inspiration aim? Is my primary purpose to deepen appreciation or to develop a general attitude? (Note knowledge and inspiration aims may be more general than a conduct response aim.)

3. Do I want this lesson to have a conduct response aim? Is my purpose to secure a specific response in daily life? If a conduct response aim is chosen, then three other questions need to be asked. Is the aim brief enough to be remembered? Is the aim clear enough to be written down? Is the aim specific enough to be attainable? A word of clarification about specificity in a conduct response aim is needed. The question of specificity of aim relates to all three types of aims, but it relates in a special way to the conduct response aim. Two further questions must be asked to determine whether the conduct response aim is sufficiently specific:

   ▲ What do I want the class members to do?

   ▲ How can they do it this week?

Now let us apply our questions to the following aim: "To seek to lead my class members to stand firm for Christ in daily relationships."

Is this a knowledge, inspiration, or conduct response aim? "To stand firm for Christ in daily relationships" sounds like a conduct response aim.

Is this aim brief enough to be remembered? Yes.

Is this aim clear enough to be written down? Yes.

Is this aim specific? No; it is too general. If someone were to ask the teacher what he wanted the class members to do, he would probably reply, "Why, I want them to stand firm for Christ, of course." If the person were to persist in asking, "But what specifically do you want your class members to do as evidence of standing firm for Christ?" It is likely the teacher would say, "There are lots of things they could do." If the person replied, "Name one!" there is a possibility the teacher would find it difficult to think of anything specific.

That is the problem. A teacher selects an aim that sounds good. In teaching the lesson he leads the group to agree in general that the aim is right (for example, that a Christian ought to stand firm for Christ). But because the teacher has no specific conduct response in mind, the class merely agrees the teacher is right but leaves the class and makes no specific response.

How can the above aim be made more specific for a class of adolescents? Here is a suggestion: "To seek to lead class members to say something helpful about the handicapped (or a racial or ethnic group) when others are speaking of them in negative terms." This is one way to express a choice to stand firm in living for Christ. (The reader might feel this is too specific. Making this aim apply to each class member will be explained later.)

Here is yet another example of an aim: "To lead class members to live a more consecrated life." If this is a conduct response aim, it is far too general. The teacher must ask the question, "What do I want the class members to do?" Then the next question must be, "How can the class members express this consecrated life this next week?" Thus, the teacher must have in mind things that the class members are not doing that they can begin to do to live a more deeply consecrated life. Almost everyone who comes to Sunday School will agree that Christians ought to live a more consecrated life. The difficulty is that so few of us do anything specifically to help us live that type of life.

We are beginning to see that one of our major teaching problems in Sunday School is that we have been teaching such vague, generalized concepts that everyone who attends Sunday School could agree with them but fail to do anything specific to carry out the ideals. For this reason, if we are to see results in Christian living, our teaching must become more specific.

5

Why Aims
Must Be Specific

How Character Develops
    Generalized Concepts
    Specific Responses
    Transfer of Training

Translating General Ideals into Specific Responses
    Identifying Specific Actions
    Words of Caution

Limited Time

Different Aims—Different Approaches

This chapter continues our discussion of the first step in a conduct response lesson plan: "Stating the aim."

It was suggested in the preceding chapter that the teacher should not have knowledge, inspiration, and conduct response aims in the same lesson. The serious teacher has asked long before now, "Why can't I have all three aims in a lesson? I don't see how anyone can teach a lesson without having some knowledge, some inspiration, and some conduct response in it." I admit this is true, but I still contend that the teacher will get better results if he or she has only one type of aim in a lesson.

You must seek that one aim as the *primary aim*. Most teachers have taught so long with only a generalized aim that they are reluctant to consider any other approach. I am not asking for immediate acceptance of this point of view. I am only asking that final judgment be withheld until the next four chapters have been read. For now I will make only a partial explanation and justification of teaching with a primary aim.

Nevertheless, I want to suggest four reasons why I think this approach is valid. The following presentation emphasizes securing results with a conduct response aim. Of course, the knowledge aim and the inspiration aim are entirely worthy and important aims. But the ultimate aim of all Christian teaching is Christian living, and today's world desperately needs Christianity in action.

How Character Develops

If teachers are to secure results in Christian living, the conduct response aim must be dominant and very specific because of the way character develops. There is considerable difference of opinion as to how character develops. What is presented here is what seems to me to be the best explanation of this complex process. Of course I recognize that the process of character development is more complex than I am picturing it here.

In what follows, an emphasis will be placed on securing change in specific areas. Yet I recognize that when an individual changes in one specific area, a whole pattern of experience changes. Current findings in psychology suggest to us that the individual responds as a whole to the total situation. Nevertheless, this emphasis on being specific in teaching is necessary to call attention to the inadequacy of traditional, generalized teaching. An attempt will be made to present this complex problem in a simplified form, trying to make it both understandable and accurate.

Generalized Concepts

Character grows out of the development of both generalized concepts and specific responses. The individual first accepts a generalized ideal such as honesty, kindness, or unselfishness as the way life ought to be lived. However, while the individual *accepts* the ideal as a whole, the ideal does not automatically operate in all the specific relationships of the person's life. Perhaps the following illustration will clarify this point.

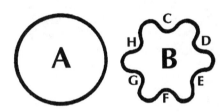

"A" is the generalized concept of honesty which the individual accepts, believing a person ought to be honest. The individual holds a certain conviction about this matter.

"B" indicates those areas of one's life (and they may be many) in which he practices this ideal of honesty. But this area does not form a perfect circle as does the general ideal, for few, if any, of us, practice a given ideal in all of our relationships.

Therefore, "C," "D," "E," and "F," and so on, indicate those areas in which the individual does not practice honesty.

For example, a respectable person would never dream of stealing money from a bank, but she might not have any qualms about stretching things a bit in making out her income tax returns. Or use the ideal of kindness. An adolescent girl may be kind to her pet cat, yet be very unkind to the new girl who has just moved into the neighborhood. While individuals hold certain generalized ideals, those ideals may or may not operate in specific situations.

It should be stated in passing that it is the function of the lesson with an inspiration-aim to develop those generalized Christian ideals and convictions out of which specific responses are to come. Inspiration is not to be minimized. It is a matter of basic importance. These ideals must be developed into convictions that are deep enough to direct decisions and control life in specific situations.

Why are generalized inspiration lessons inadequate for Christian teaching? In the first place, experience has indicated that specific responses do not automatically follow the acceptance of a generalized ideal. In the second place, Christian conviction does not automatically give Christian insight to an individual. A husband may deeply desire to be Christian in his family relationships but that does not tell him automatically how many times a month he should take his wife out to dinner, nor does it tell him the proper way to discipline his children. Judged by the way that some preachers neglect their families, it seems they are more unchristian in their homes than in almost any other area. It also may well be that others are just as guilty as preachers.

Specific Responses

If it is true that it is not sufficient merely to lead an individual to accept a general Christian ideal, then how can individuals apply these ideals in areas where they need to be practiced? Or, rather, how can these specific relationships and situations be brought under the control and direction of the ideal?

In Sunday School class sessions, specific areas must be lifted to the level of consciousness. Class members must be made aware of their failure to express properly their own ideal. The Scriptures are used to throw light on the problem; the members share their ideas, problems, and experiences. The teacher guides the discussion, contributing insights and experiences. In this process the Holy Spirit has an opportunity to convict each individual of sin (or shortcomings). If this conviction is sufficiently deep, class members will change their practices to conform to the ideal. This is conduct response.

It is not sufficient for the teacher to continue to have general aims like these:

▲ To lead my class to be more honest,

▲ To lead my class to be more kind,

▲ To lead my class to be more missionary minded.

Rather, the teacher must lift out one specific area in which the class has a need, such as these:

▲ To lead my class to be more honest in (a specific area),

▲ To lead my class to be more kind in (a specific relationship),

▲ To lead my class to be more missionary minded by (a specific response).

If each individual in the class has a different need, adapt the aim to each individual, but be specific for each. For a group of adolescents, an aim might be: "To seek to lead my class to make their homes happier places by (1) keeping their rooms straight, or (2) hanging up their clothes, (3) making up their beds, (4) mowing the grass, or (5) drying the dishes."[1]

Each individual in the class could select the specific response she needs most to make her home happier. The point is, *teaching in general terms is inadequate for securing conduct response.* Rather, a person's need lies in those specific areas where he or she now needs to practice these ideals.

Is there a danger that this type of teaching might become too personal? Will some members be offended? That depends on the teacher. If he uses good judgment, if he has good rapport with the class, and if he demonstrates that he is seeking to do that which he is teaching, a large part of the problem will be solved. Then, it should be understood that conduct response teaching is based on a conversion experience in which the learner indicates that his or her deepest desire is to know and follow the will of God and the teachings of Jesus. This teaching tries to help the individual discover what the Christian life means in specific situations and specific relationships. If properly conducted by the teacher, there is no reason for a learner to be offended. It is simply Christianity in action.

Some may object that these visible results might become mere pharisaical observances that are purely mechanical or outward responses in the life of the individual. This danger always con-

---

1. The teacher must understand that these specific responses do not become the focus of discussion in the development of the lesson. These specific responses are not mentioned until the portion of the lesson called "Carry-over" or perhaps one may be used in the part of the lesson plan called "Making the Lesson Personal."

fronts experiential and spiritual religion. A spiritual motivation is the only adequate motivation for any Christian action. However, the alternatives are not to have outward expression without spiritual motivation on the one hand or spiritual motivation without outward expression on the other. The ideal is to have Christian action based on spiritual motivation. It is the responsibility of the teacher to keep spiritual motivation dominant in the decisions of the class members.

By analyzing life situations, teachers help class members develop insights that will change their lives. The class members already accept a generalized concept, but they have no specific insights. The teacher helps class members develop this insight, but it involves more than the teacher:

▲ The Scriptures shed light on the problem.

▲ Other class members share their insights and experiences.

▲ The Holy Spirit guides individuals.

At last the individual comes to the place where he says inwardly: "I see it! I understand it! This is right!" This insight is life-changing. It is not mechanical but is based on conviction of sin and on the conviction that a given course of action is right. The spiritual motivation is still basic.

Transfer of Training

The question might be raised, Does this approach mean we must deal with every specific response in a person's experience before he can develop a Christian character? The answer is no, but this question suggests the issue of transfer of training. It is possible for those things a person learns in one situation to transfer and influence his or her response in another situation *under certain conditions*. However, this transfer is not automatic.

At least four factors help determine whether things learned in one situation will transfer and affect another situation. Consider these four questions:

1. Are there common elements in the learner's new situation and the learner's past experiences?

2. To what extent is the learner aware of these common elements?

3. How deep is the learner's conviction in this particular area?

4. How strong are the other influences pulling the learner in the new situation?

Let's take a situation and see how these four factors would affect transfer of training. Say that an eight-year-old boy is given the correct change to ride the city bus to town. In getting on the bus with a large group of people, he forgets to put in his fare. So many people are getting on at the same time that the bus driver does not notice the omission. Just after the boy sits down, he feels in his pocket and finds the change he was given. The boy has been taught the general ideal of honesty. In other experiences, he has been taught that he should not take money from his mother's purse, that he should not pick up apples in the grocery store, and that he should not take a pencil from another person's desk at school. What will he do in this new situation? Will his past learning transfer and influence his response in this situation?

Now let's apply our four questions to the boy on the bus. The four factors do not come in any particular order, but let's follow the order given above.

First question: Are there common elements in the boy's new situation and his past experiences? His earlier experiences in the areas of forgiveness or neatness will not affect this new situation he faces because there are no common elements. But he has had certain experiences validating the importance of honesty, and there are elements in the new problem he faces in common with his past experiences. So there is the possibility that past experiences may affect his response—or they may not.

Second question: To what extent is the boy aware of these common elements? As adults, we are able to see them easily, but the child's failure to see that not paying his fare is the same as taking money from a cash register will influence his response. On the other hand, the child might come home later and say, "Mother, I didn't have to pay my fare today." "Why?" the mother might ask. "Because I forgot to put it in." The mother might then reply with some feeling, "Son, don't you know that's wrong? That's just the same as stealing." And the child might innocently reply, "Mother, I didn't know it was wrong. I didn't know it was stealing." That is, he saw no connection at all between his failure to give the bus driver his fare and his past experiences in the area of honesty. If this were the case, his past experiences would not affect his response. There would be no transfer.

Third question: How deep is the boy's conviction about honesty? If he has developed an intense revulsion toward dishonesty and a deep, inner desire to be honest, his response will be correspondingly influenced. On the other hand, the child may be aware of the common elements; he may know that not paying his fare is wrong. But if he has no depth of conviction about honesty or the evils of stealing he may say to himself, "I don't care. I'm going to keep the money anyway." His conviction was not sufficiently strong to influence his response. This is a factor of no little importance, not only on a child level but also on an adult level. There are many who know they ought to do certain things (they ought to go to church, they ought to go to Sunday School, they ought to endeavor to improve their community, and so on), but they stop there. Their conviction in these particular areas is not very deep, at least not deep enough to call forth corresponding action.

Fourth question: How strong are the other influences pulling the boy in the new situation? Perhaps the child is aware of the common elements and has very strong convictions concerning honesty. But, he may think how nice it would be to use this money to buy an ice cream cone. It is entirely possible that the desire for the ice cream cone might outweigh all other factors and be the "pull" which determines his response.

How will the child respond? It will depend on which of these four factors are the strongest in his particular situation. A person's acceptance and practice of the ideal of honesty in certain situations does not mean that this learning will transfer automatically and operate in all other situations. Neither does this mean that transfer of training cannot take place. It does mean two things: (1) that we must seek to lead class members to have the deepest possible convictions; and (2) that we must deal in specific responses, helping individuals to see the relation of one particular response to as many other similar responses as possible.

Translating General Ideals into Specific Responses

We have already mentioned the difficulty people have in translating general ideals into specific responses. What does it mean to be thoroughly Christian in our business relations? Surely, to follow the spirit of Jesus in business involves more than just being honest and courteous. However, people in business often find it difficult to extend this ideal to other specific responses.

Identifying Specific Actions

Suppose the teacher of a class of young women has just written out the following aim for a lesson: "To seek to lead my class to express their love for Jesus in their everyday relationships." Now let's apply our test questions from pages 57 and 58 to this aim.

▲ Is this a knowledge, an inspiration, or a conduct response aim? The teacher answers, "I intend for it to be a conduct response aim."

▲ Is it brief enough to be remembered? We agree that it is.

▲ Is it clear enough to be written down? Again, we agree that it is.

▲ Is it specific? The teacher replies, "Of course, it is." But, really, is it sufficiently specific?

To test whether it is specific we must ask the teacher two more questions:

▲ If it is a specific conduct response you are seeking, what do you want your class to do? The teacher replies, "I want them to express their love for Jesus in their daily lives."

▲ How can they express it? What specific actions must they take?

Suppose the teacher has taught this lesson using the above stated aim. After the class, one of the young women comes to the teacher and says: "This was a wonderful lesson. I was really convicted. I want to do as you suggested and try to express my love for Jesus in my daily life. What should I start doing *that I am not doing now* to express this love?" What would the teacher say?

One pivotal part of the above question is the phrase "that I am not now doing." Usually in a class where the teacher challenges us to practice some Christian ideal (or in the worship where the pastor challenges us regarding some ideal), our tendency is to think of those places in our lives where we are already expressing the ideal. Then, like Little Jack Horner, we stick in our thumb and pull out a plum and say, "What a good person am I."

There are two possible responses the teacher might make to the class member's question. One is, "I don't know." This would be a tragic answer, but some teachers would have to make such a confession. Another possible response might be, "There are many ways you might express that love." True, but what is one thing that young woman is not now doing that she should start doing immediately? Some teachers will have difficulty thinking of something specific. If that is true they can be sure that, more than likely, class members will not think of anything specific either.

Probably, they will simply agree with the teacher's generalized aim and go on living just as they have been. Psychologists tell us that we change our lives in specific areas. We seldom change in general ones. In other words, we do not normally become good all over.

The teacher needs to know the class members so intimately that he will recognize some particular area where they are failing to express their love for Jesus. Then, in the carry-over section of the lesson plan, he may direct the thinking of the class to this area and the members can discuss it openly and frankly. The Holy Spirit will have a chance to work within them in some specific way. If conviction is deep enough, the individual will change his or her way of living, and the teacher will have had a part in bringing about a conduct response.

Words of Caution

Two words of caution should be given to this emphasis on being specific in the area of conduct response.

Some will object. In spite of protestations to the contrary, the members of a class may not like this emphasis. That is, they may not be willing to make specific changes in their lives. We have come to be comfortable with our lives. While we all confess that we need to improve our Christian lives, some of us are not ready to do as much as we might think.

Let me share an example from a comic strip. Those of you who follow "Beetle Bailey" by Mort Walker may remember this.[2] First frame: Sarge comes up on Beetle Bailey who is sitting against a building asleep. Next frame: Sarge blasts him as a blankety-blank

---

2. *The (Orlando) Sentinel,* September 22, 1992.

goof-off. Beetle says, "Sarge, you generalize too much." Next frame: Beetle continues, "How can I ever improve until you tell me specifically what I've done wrong?" Next frame: Sarge says, "Okay, you need a haircut, your shirt is dirty, button's off . . ." Next frame: Sarge continues, "There was dust on your footlocker, your bed was unmade, gum under your shelf . . ." Next frame: Sarge continues, "A book was upside down, a coat hanger facing the wrong way, your bed a half-inch off line, thumbprints on your shoes . . ." Next frame: Beetle replies, "Y'know Sarge, I liked you better when you generalized." Unfortunately, we all are a lot like Beetle.

Don't expect automatic results. My second word of caution is this: The teacher should not expect automatic results because he has a specific conduct response aim. Even when we do our best, some class members will make no desirable change. The Holy Spirit is still the great Teacher. But, like the farmer, we must cooperate intelligently with God and provide the most favorable conditions for Him to do His effective work. We will have a better chance to secure specific conduct response in life when we have a specific conduct response aim in mind than if we have only a general aim in mind.

Limited Time

There is a very practical reason why it is unwise to try to achieve all three types of aims in one lesson. The time we have for teaching is very limited. When we have a knowledge aim in mind, we must seek to stimulate interest on the part of the class in the material to be learned. Motivation that is deep enough to result in serious study must be aroused. The knowledge to be learned must be presented or discovered. Elaboration, drill, repetition, and review must follow to make the learning last. It takes time to teach for knowledge and teach it well.

The same is true in pursuing an inspiration aim. It takes time to lead people in the study of an ideal or attitude in which their emotions are stirred, their appreciations are heightened, and their convictions are deepened. Certainly, it takes time to secure conduct response. At best, people are reluctant to change. It is not easy to induce people to exclude certain things from their lives that have become habitual or to begin practicing certain Christian virtues that have not been a part of their normal experience.

Thus, thinking in terms of the time factor alone, it becomes obvious that the teacher faces an almost impossible task when trying to achieve all three aims in one lesson.

Different Aims—Different Approaches

The teacher should use a different approach for each of these three types of aims. Suppose the aim is to lead the class to learn the significant facts about Paul's first missionary journey. The teacher would use a quite different approach if the aim was to lead class members to be more missionary minded or to engage in a missionary project. If the teacher has selected a conduct response aim, she will certainly have to use a certain amount of knowledge, but she will not be using the methods of teaching that lead to a mastery of knowledge as such. The approach to be used in securing conduct response is very different from the approach a teacher would use in seeking an inspiration aim or a knowledge aim. The next four chapters will provide an elaboration and explanation of this statement.

Let me close by stating again that all three teaching aims are valid. My emphasis in the next four chapters is on conduct response. The inspiration aim and the knowledge aim are also entirely worthy. There is a time and a place for each of the three aims. But each aim requires a different approach. We are presenting the approach that we believe should be used in securing conduct response.

6

Securing
Purposeful Bible Study

Preparing the Class to Read the Bible
>   Arouse Class Members' Interest and Curiosity
>   Tell Class Members What to Look For
>   Ask Class Members for Answers

An Illustration

An Analysis of the Illustration
>   Arouse Interest and Curiosity
>   Tell Class Members What to Look For
>   Ask Class Members for Answers

Eight Mistakes Teachers Should Avoid
>   The Dull Plan
>   The Poor Transition
>   The Overloaded Introduction
>   The Complicated Introduction
>   Bible Reading Without Questions
>   Poorly Graded Questions
>   Questions Unrelated to the Lesson Aim
>   Too Many Questions

Examples of How to Secure Purposeful Bible Study
>   Psalm 100
>   Luke 1:1–4
>   Romans 7:4–25

We have spent two chapters examining how to state an aim. This is step 1 of a conduct response lesson plan.[1] Now we will discuss step 2 of the lesson plan, "How to secure purposeful Bible study."

This discussion centers on what we generally call the introduction to the lesson. In this chapter we want to find principles that will help us arouse the interest of the class and create in it a desire to read the Bible text on which the lesson is based. This chapter is *not* a study of how the Bible may be used in developing the lesson.

Many teachers begin the class session on Sunday morning by reading the Scripture suggested for the lesson. But this reading does not usually arouse within the members a sense of holy expectancy and does not elicit from them an enthusiastic response. Why? Probably because the teacher has not yet aroused within class members a genuine desire to read the Scriptures.

Some classes don't even use the Bible, only the quarterly. In other classes the teacher is the only one who brings a Bible. The members never bring their Bibles because they never have occasion to use them.

In still other classes, the Bible is used but not effectively. The teacher makes little or no effort to stimulate the members' interest in reading it. The teacher assumes that because the Bible is being read the members automatically will listen. In some adult classes a member of the class is asked to read the Scripture passage. The reader stumbles through the text without giving meaning to the Scripture, and the class members sit there thinking about something else.

Often, teachers of adolescents ask each member to read one verse of the Scripture passage. This ensures participation, but it doesn't guarantee purposeful Bible study. Usually, while the first two or three members are reading, the others silently read the verses they will have to read aloud later. After reading the assigned verse, each participant relaxes and ignores the verses classmates are reading. Here again, the Bible is not used effectively.

After an unfamiliar portion of Scripture is read in the average Sunday School class, few class members can explain what is in the passage. If we want to magnify the Bible in our Sunday Schools, let's find out how to make it meaningful and significant.

---

1. All five steps of a conduct response lesson plan are given on page 135.

Preparing the Class to Read the Bible

How can the teacher secure the attention of the class? How can this attention be deepened into interest? How can she help class members want to open the Bible to see what it has to say about the problem to be studied in the lesson? Teachers must consider these questions in planning the introduction to the lesson.

The Scripture passage is usually read at the beginning of the lesson, but sometimes it is better to delay the Scripture reading until the middle of the teaching period. At other times, parts of the passage can be read throughout the lesson period. No method guarantees serious and meaningful study, but the following three-step method works for many teachers.

Step #1: Arouse Class Members' Interest and Curiosity

Here is a general rule: Do not read the Bible as the first thing done in the class period. Read the Bible only after class members are ready for it. But when are they ready for Bible reading? Only after the teacher has aroused within the class members a desire to want to know what the Scripture passage says. If Bible study is to be purposeful, the group must have a reason for studying it. Their curiosity must be aroused. Their attention must be focused. By using well-chosen questions or statements to begin the lesson, the teacher arouses such a deep interest in the members that they want to study the particular passage.

Another question naturally follows: How can I arouse this interest in the members? Here are four simple suggestions:

1. Your introduction should be in line with the interests of the group. Whatever you say in your opening statement should appeal to the interests of the members. They will pay attention only if they are interested in the subject. If the teacher of adolescent boys begins a lesson talking about Shallum and Menahem, kings of the Northern Kingdom of Israel, he will probably find the boys restless and disinterested. On the other hand, if the teacher begins by referring to the baseball game which the boys saw (or played) Saturday afternoon, he will have their attention immediately. Even though the primary purpose of the Sunday School is to study the Bible, the teacher must not assume that class members will automatically be interested and give rapt attention.

In determining how to prepare a group for purposeful Bible study, the teacher should always keep in mind that the purpose in these opening statements is to arouse the members' curiosity. She wants to raise questions in their minds. She want them to do some thinking of their own. There are many ways of accomplishing this:

▲ Carefully planned questions

▲ Unusual or striking statements

▲ Stories or illustrations

▲ Newspaper clippings

▲ Magazine articles

▲ Pictures

One Sunday when the lesson was on drinking, one teacher of adults cut out some lavishly colored magazine advertisements for alcoholic beverages. He pasted them end to end and rolled them into a big roll. On Sunday morning, he began the lesson by saying, "Look what I found in some magazines last week!" Then he unrolled it before the class. Eight feet of liquor advertisements seized everyone's attention, and the teacher easily directed their thinking to the relevant Scripture passage.

Regardless of the method of introduction, the teacher should await some vocal response from the group before beginning the Bible reading. This expression from the class concentrates their attention and deepens their interest.

2. Keep your introduction in line with the lesson aim. It is not enough for the teacher to secure attention by talking about something in which the class might be interested. Any teacher can interest adolescent boys in yesterday's ball game. But can he lead their interest beyond the ball game to the lesson? The teacher's introduction must do both. It must be in line with the interests of the group, but it must also be in line with the lesson aim.

3. Use a natural transition. In the example given above, the teacher's possible difficulty in moving into the lesson can be avoided if the transition from the ball game to reading the Scripture is carefully planned. The transition is crucial. Without it, the class will continue in idle talk, discussing any item of interest. The teacher must get their attention but then lead them to an intelligent reading of the Scripture.

Step #2: Tell Class Members What to Look For

When the teacher has stimulated the interest of his class in line with the purpose of the lesson, he will then be ready to take the second step in his effort to secure purposeful study of the Bible. He must guide the class members' reading of the Scripture by telling them what to be looking for in the Bible passage while it is being read. This focuses their attention on the most important things for the lesson. It gives the class both purpose and direction in its study.

I have often read an unfamiliar portion of Scripture to groups of teachers. After the reading, I asked one or two simple questions based on the passage. Rarely have these teachers been able to answer them. They always say, "Read it again." When I ask why they want it read again, the group replies, "We know what to look for now." This experience has taught me that *the teacher should tell the class in advance what to look for as the passage is read.*

You will usually have best results when you point out what to look for by asking a question. Sometimes I ask two or three questions, but three is about as many as they can remember. It helps if you write these on the chalkboard. In any case, make sure everybody clearly understands them.

It isn't always necessary to ask questions. Sometimes the teacher may simply say, "I would like for you to note the following things as the Scripture passage is read." The teacher will think of other variations that might be used.

Step #3: Ask Class Members for Answers

After the Scripture passage is read, asking class members for the answers to the questions previously asked helps the class in two ways:

▲ The teacher makes sure that class members have found the right answers. We often assume that our members know more than they actually do. Vocal answers to the questions help the teacher make sure the members did not get some mistaken idea or allow him or her to clear up some confusing point.

▲ Class members recognize that the teacher really means for them to look for the answer. If the teacher asks the class to find the answer to a question or questions but never again raises the questions, the members soon ignore such requests.

Asking and answering these questions leads naturally into discussion or the development of the lesson.

An Illustration

Let's eavesdrop as a class of young adult men study a lesson with this aim: "To lead my class members into a deeper appreciation of Jesus as the divine Son of God." (This is an inspiration aim.)

TEACHER (at the beginning of the lesson): Does the name David Koresh mean anything to you? (The tragedy with Koresh and the Branch Davidians transpired shortly before this was written.)

RESPONSE: He was the leader of that cult group out in Waco.

TEACHER: Did Koresh really claim to be God?

RESPONSE: I don't know. I didn't read all that stuff.

RESPONSE: Boy, I did. The paper said Koresh wrote a letter and signed it, "Yahweh Koresh."[2]

TEACHER: Surely those who followed him must have been uneducated people?

RESPONSE: I saw on TV an interview with a man who said his sister was out there. He seemed to be well-educated.

RESPONSE: I heard that one of his followers was a graduate of Harvard.

TEACHER: What do you think of David Koresh?

RESPONSE: I think he was a fake!

RESPONSE: Yeah, he was nuts!

TEACHER: What would you have thought of Jesus if you had been living when Jesus was on earth in the flesh?

For a moment the class sits in silence pondering what their attitude might have been in light of what they have just been saying. Finally, one of the members speaks.

RESPONSE: I am not sure.

RESPONSE: I've sometimes thought about that.

RESPONSE: But Jesus' teachings were so different!

---

2. *The (Orlando) Sentinel*, April 11, 1993, A3.

RESPONSE: Evidently Koresh's teachings appealed to his followers, too!

RESPONSE: Man, that's a tough one.

TEACHER: What did the people of Jesus' day think of Him? Let's turn to the twelfth chapter of John and find out what their reaction was. As we read verses 12 through 19 and 35 through 43, look for the answers to the following questions:

▲ What was the reaction of the masses of the people?

▲ What was the reaction of the Pharisees?

▲ What was the reaction of some of the chief rulers?

At this point, everyone in the class opens their Bibles, and the teacher reads the Scripture.

After reading the Scripture, the teacher asks, "What was the reaction of the masses of the people?" The class responds. The teacher moves on to the other two questions and then leads naturally into the discussion of the lesson.

An Analysis of the Illustration

Now let us analyze this illustration in light of our three principles.

Arouse Interest and Curiosity

Our first principle stated that the teacher must arouse the interest and curiosity of the class to the point that they have a desire to study the Bible passage.

To arouse interest and curiosity, the teacher's opening must be in line with the interests of the group. The name and actions of David Koresh had been in the news so much that everyone was familiar with his name, and they were even curious about what would happen next. The questions that followed were designed to deepen their interest and stimulate thought.

To secure and deepen the attention of the class, there must be a normal transition from the opening discussion to the problem to be discussed in the lesson. The transition in the above illustration is in the two questions, "If you had lived at the time when Jesus was on earth, what would you have thought of Him?" and "What did the people of Jesus' day think of Him?" The class might have been interested in pursuing the discussion of David Koresh further, but these questions immediately turned the thinking of the group away from David Koresh toward Jesus. The transition was so natural that the group almost immediately forgot about Koresh.

The approach the teacher uses to secure attention and lead into a purposeful study of the Scripture must also be in line with the aim for the lesson. The question, "What did the people of His day think about Him?" is closely related to the lesson.

Tell Class Members What to Look For

The second principle suggested was that the class be told what to look for. The teacher in the illustration asked three questions. Note that each question was in line with the lesson aim: to lead my class members into a deeper appreciation of Jesus as the divine Son of God.

Ask Class Members for Answers

At this point, the Scripture passage was read and the teacher asked for answers to his questions. Asking and answering the questions led into the development of the lesson.

Eight Mistakes Teachers Should Avoid

I have used this plan with teachers for several years, and I have discovered the eight mistakes teachers most often make. Maybe this list will help you avoid them.

Mistake #1: The Dull Plan

Often the teacher's plan to secure group interest is not stimulating enough. The more dramatic or intriguing you can make this phase of the lesson, the better it will be. The ideal or goal of the teacher should be to arouse the curiosity and interest of the group enough to awaken a genuine desire to open the Bible and see what it has to say. This is not an easy goal to achieve, but it is the one toward which the teacher should strive.

Mistake #2: The Poor Transition

Too often the teacher fails to plan a normal transition that leads from the interest-getting phase of the introduction to the problem to be considered in the lesson. Because of this failure to have a good transition, the teacher often finds it difficult to lead naturally into the discussion of the lesson. The class continues to talk about the item of interest the teacher has suggested, and the teacher can think of no way to get them off this topic and into the lesson. This wastes important time in idle, useless talk. This transition is important, and it must be carefully planned.

Mistake #3: The Overloaded Introduction

In his or her introduction the teacher must not tell the class what is in the Scripture passage. The teacher's task is to lead them to want to know what is in the passage. Telling the class what is in the Scripture does not stimulate the class to study the Scripture nor give them a purpose for studying it.

Mistake #4: The Complicated Introduction

Sometimes the teacher gets too involved in trying to work out a plan to secure purposeful Bible study. Do not let your plan be long, involved, or complex. Be as specific and simple as possible.

Mistake #5: Bible Reading Without Questions

The teacher often forgets to give the class some questions for which they are to find answers as the Scripture passage is read. This is an important part of the whole process. If we are going to lead our class to study the Bible with a purpose, we must tell them specifically what to look for. This will direct their study.

Mistake #6: Poorly Graded Questions

The questions must be on the age level of the class being taught. If the teacher has a group of adults, he would not want to ask them to look for the answers to questions that are so simple it would insult their intelligence. If the teacher has a class of adolescents, he would not want to ask such difficult questions that they would be unable to find the answers. Without being too difficult, the questions should challenge the minds of class members, whatever their ages.

Mistake #7: Questions Unrelated to the Lesson Aim

Sometimes the questions posed are not related to the teacher's aim for the lesson. They should have some relation to the aim so that answering them will lead naturally from the introduction to the development of the lesson.

Mistake #8: Too Many Questions

Sometimes the teacher tells the group to look for answers to too many questions. Don't overload the group. Limit questions to two or three.

Over the years as I have taught these principles in conferences, the question teachers asked most often regarding this section of the lesson plan was, "Assuming the teacher has 'properly prepared' the class members for the Scripture reading, who should actually read the Bible aloud, the teacher or the members?" Here, as elsewhere, variety is the best approach. However, since I have some rather strong feelings at this point let me make the following comments. Whenever the Bible is read, it should be *read well!* It should be read so that the listeners will be able to understand its *meaning.* This means the one who reads will need to have read the verses before the class session and probably will have practiced reading them in order to read smoothly and communicate the proper meaning of the passage. Unfortunately a lot of teachers (and pastors) need help and practice at this point. For this reason I feel strongly the teacher should be the one who reads the Scripture passage in this part of the lesson. And it will help greatly if the teacher and the class members use a modern translation. I feel the class will get far more out of the reading of the Scripture if they are following along, looking for answers to questions the teacher has posed. This is neither the best time nor the best way to secure participation by the members. Later in the development of the lesson and in other parts of the lesson plan the members will ask questions, discuss, and read the Bible.

Examples of How to Secure Purposeful Bible Study

Psalm 100

This example was prepared by a layperson who teaches in a church in Louisville. The age of her class was not given but I assume it was a group of high school girls. The teacher's aim for this lesson: "To seek to lead my class members to attend the morning worship service each Sunday this quarter." (This is a conduct response aim.)

TEACHER: How many of you play some kind of musical instrument?

RESPONSES: I do (with some telling what instrument they played) or I don't.

TEACHER: What type of music do you like best?

RESPONSES: Heavy rock. Soft rock. (Other such responses.)

TEACHER: If you were playing in a band that was going to play for the president of the United States and you were appointed to choose the music, what would you choose?

RESPONSES: Patriotic music. Something that features the saxophone because he plays the saxophone.

TEACHER: In other words, you would select something appropriate for the occasion or something the president liked. Are all people's taste in music alike?

RESPONSE: I should say not! My folks hate heavy metal!

TEACHER: Does God like music or singing?

RESPONSE: I suppose so.

TEACHER: Get your Bibles and turn to Psalm 100. As I read, I want you to find the answer to three questions. (The teacher writes the following questions on the chalkboard.)

▲ What kind of music does God like? (Joyful)

▲ When we enter the worship service, what should we give God? (Thanksgiving and praise)

▲ What has He given us?" (Mercy and faithfulness)

Luke 1:1–4

A former student of mine prepared this for a lesson plan with a knowledge aim. This example illustrates the fact that this approach also can be used with a knowledge aim lesson. She stated her lesson aim in these words: "To seek to lead the class members to master some major facts about the writing of each of the four Gospels."

The teacher brings to class with her four pictures of the same person taken at different times and in different places.

TEACHER: (showing the four pictures to the members of her class) What do these pictures have in common?

RESPONSE: They are pictures of the same person.

TEACHER: In what ways are the pictures different?

RESPONSES: They were taken at different places. The person has on different clothes. Only two of them were taken outdoors.

TEACHER: What are some reasons they are different?

RESPONSES: They were taken at different times. One of them was taken by a professional photographer. The person is wearing different clothes in each picture.

TEACHER: But we agree they are all of the same person. Can we get an idea of that person's personality through these four pictures? If so, how?

RESPONSES: She is athletic, because she is playing tennis in one picture. Another shows her at a party!

TEACHER: We have four "photographs" of Jesus available to us. We call them the four Gospels. None is more valid or better than the others, but they each present the life and ministry of Jesus from a different perspective. Luke the physician gives a very brief statement about why he wrote his Gospel. Turn to Luke 1, verse 1, and as I read, find the answers to the following questions:

1. Were the Books of Matthew, Mark, Luke, and John the only accounts of the life of Jesus that were written? (No, Luke said there were "many.")

2. What was one thing Luke said he wanted to do? (He wanted to write his account down in order.)

3. What was Luke's reason for writing? ("That thou mightest know the certainty of those things, wherein thou hast been instructed" [KJV])

Romans 7:4–25

This was also prepared by a student for a class of young adults. The teacher's aim is this: "To seek to lead my class to deepen their inner spiritual life by: (1) beginning the practice of reading the Bible daily, or (2) having daily prayer with another person, or (3) starting a discussion and prayer group at the office, or (4) choosing another similar action to produce the same result."

TEACHER: Who can tell me what is meant by a split personality?

RESPONSE: It is a person who shows two different personalities at different times.

TEACHER: Right! In fact, it can be more than two personalities in the same body. Who is the most famous "split personality" you know either in reality or fiction?

RESPONSE: Dr. Jekyll and Mr. Hyde.

TEACHER: Good! Tell me, what do you think it would be like to have a split personality?

RESPONSE: I wouldn't like it. I'm having a hard enough time trying to be me.

TEACHER: When we think of Dr. Jekyll and Mr. Hyde, we think of a split personality as being bad. But did you know the apostle Paul considered himself as having a split personality?

RESPONSE: I don't believe it! You're kidding!

TEACHER: Let's turn to Romans 7. I will begin reading at verse 15 and I want you to find the answers to these two questions:

▲ Which verse best points out to you Paul's conflict in his life? (Responses may vary. Let a couple of men read the verse they chose to support their answers.)

▲ How did Paul say he felt about this conflict? (He felt wretched.)

Let this concluding word be said. A teacher will not always use this method exactly as suggested here. Any plan can get monotonous. Teachers must vary their procedures, but the same principles are used whatever the variation.

7

Developing the Lesson

Why Lesson Development?
    Understanding the Scripture Passage
    Building Christian Attitudes
    Committing to a Christian Attitude

Arranging Content in Lesson Development
    Arrangement by Topic
    Arrangement by Attitude

An Illustration of Both Approaches
    The Logical Arrangement
    The Psychological Arrangement

To Summarize
    Teacher's Self-examination
    Using Bible Content
    The Teacher's Attitude

The third step in a conduct response lesson plan is developing the lesson. This portion of the lesson takes the most class time on Sunday morning. And for most teachers it also requires the most preparation time. We are now considering the conduct response aim.

Later in this book we will consider how to plan a lesson with a knowledge aim. The suggested approach to developing the knowledge aim lesson is radically different from the approach we will outline in this chapter.

Why Lesson Development?

Each part of a lesson plan has a purpose. The aim serves a purpose. The introduction serves a purpose. But what is the purpose of the section of the lesson plan we call developing the lesson? The reader is probably thinking, "Everybody knows that. That's where we share with the class the spiritual truths in the Scripture passage." Certainly this is true. But this statement is much too vague and too general. (This is the same problem we met when seeking to make our lesson aim sufficiently specific.) Let me try to explain what I mean by the purpose of developing the lesson.

Of course the general purpose of lesson development is *to help achieve the lesson aim*. Obvious though the above purpose may be, it is nearly always violated! I have visited many Sunday School classes across America. Many teachers seem more concerned to cover the material in the Scripture passage than they are to accomplish an identifiable aim.

Building on this general purpose, there are at least three specific purposes for development of the lesson which the teacher should seek to accomplish. Each of these three is very important.

Purpose #1: Understanding the Scripture Passage

In lesson development, the teacher should seek to lead class members to have some understanding of the meaning of the Scripture passage. I have already said that teachers often seem more concerned to cover the Scripture passage than to accomplish an identifiable aim. Yet teachers should be deeply concerned with helping the class have *some understanding* of the Scripture that is the basis of the lesson. How much understanding should the teacher seek? This depends on how much time the teacher needs for other parts of the lesson plan. Also, the teacher must remember that understanding the Scripture passage is only one of three things necessary to fulfilling the purpose of lesson development.

Purpose #2: Building Christian Attitudes

The second purpose the teacher should seek in lesson development is to lead the members to understand the Christian attitude upon which the aim is based. Obviously, every Christian conduct response is based on a general Christian attitude. I recommend the teacher *identify the attitude.* Put it in words! Give it a name—honesty. Or describe it—to be more loving. Remember that an attitude is a generalized concept. In the lesson plan the teacher should write the name of the attitude alongside the section heading, Lesson Development. The teacher should identify and write down this Christian attitude to clarify just what she wants class members to understand.

Two questions will help you plan how to build Christian attitudes in lesson development.

What basic teachings or insights are given in the Scripture passage relating to the Christian attitude? You should write these down because they will be the best part of lesson development. Later in your lesson development you will decide how to use these in developing the lesson. For now, you are simply identifying them.

Are there other insights in other passages in the Bible that need to be considered in understanding the Christian attitude? Of course, time in class will be so limited that we will necessarily omit some spiritual lessons in the printed Scripture. These are all important truths, but God has impressed upon us to seek a specific conduct response in the lives of our class members. Therefore, in the following lesson, focus on developing the attitude rather than trying to explain every verse suggested by the lesson.

Yet in seeking a conduct response aim, we must consider the teachings of the whole Bible about that response. This is basic. Again, time will be a limiting factor, but insofar as time will allow, the teacher should lead the class members to confront and consider some of the biblical teachings not included in a given lesson. In planning the lesson, the teacher should think about each member of the class and then himself, asking "What part of the biblical teaching do the members need most to study about this attitude? Asking this question will help the teacher know where to place the focus.

Purpose #3: Committing to a Christian Attitude

The lesson development should lead members to begin the process of commitment to the new attitude. The teacher should note that two of the three purposes of lesson development deal with the Christian attitude underlying the desired conduct response. This points up the importance of teachers having the new Christian attitude clearly in mind and writing it down; otherwise, the teacher will be unable to work out lesson development as it should be done.

Remember, at this point the teacher is alone with God planning the lesson. In seeking to lead class members toward a deepening commitment to the attitude, the teacher should ask two questions.

What problems will class members face if they express this new attitude in some part of their lives? What problems, difficulties, and temptations come to them from outside of themselves? This depends upon the age of those being taught. This is also why the teacher needs to know class members intimately and develop a caring, trusting relationship with them. Is the class a group of adult women, including single mothers, full-time homemakers, and wives working outside the home? Is the class a group of youth in high school, facing peer pressure, drugs, and conflicts of numerous types? Whatever the age and whatever the circumstances, class members today face a wide variety of problems. The teacher must help them face these problems and relate them to the teachings of Holy Scripture.

What "hang-ups" might class members have? Hang-ups are difficulties that come from within us. We have already had experiences with people of other races, and these experiences have formed our attitude toward these races. We have already worked by certain practices in business relations that have become a part of the pattern of our lives.

When the teacher of a large Sunday School class interprets a passage in a way that conflicts with a basic, existing attitude, what do most class members do? Most silently reject it or ignore it because over the years, we have learned how to build a shield around ourselves.

What happens in a small Sunday School class with a relationship of openness and honesty? The teacher has an opportunity, carefully and lovingly, to seek to lead each member to identify and evaluate (privately or vocally as each may choose) their very real and difficult hang-ups. Members of a small class are more likely to struggle with the biblical attitude being studied.

Arranging Content in Lesson Development

Now that we understand clearly the three purposes of lesson development, how does the teacher arrange the content he plans to use in this part of the lesson plan? Please understand, I am not asking what method or methods should be used. This is an important question, but methodology is not our concern at this time. Earlier it was said that lesson development often is referred to as the body of the lesson. This means it includes the major portion of the content. The question for the teacher here is, for a lesson with a conduct response aim, what content should be used and how will that content be arranged? Undoubtedly there are numerous approaches to arranging the content in lesson development. I would like to examine and give my evaluation of two of these approaches.

Arrangement by Topic

Preachers strive to arrange the content of a Scripture passage in the most logical manner possible. This arrangement by topic is *logical arrangement*. Teachers often use logical arrangement in lesson development. They divide the Scripture passage into two, three, or more major points to use in developing the lesson. They identify subpoints to elaborate and clarify each of the major points in the outline. Sometimes they even add subpoints to the subpoints.

An even more popular form of logical arrangement is verse-by-verse exposition. I have found in visiting churches that most teachers use this approach. The teacher knows that most of the study helps in the teacher's quarterly are verse-by-verse exposition. Most teachers deeply appreciate this exposition because they have little serious Bible knowledge. Any help they can get is a real help.

Here is a verse-by-verse approach to lesson development based on the Beatitudes. The printed Scripture passage is Matthew 5:1–12. Most teachers love to teach this lesson because it is full of truths to emphasize. They teach verse by verse, taking the truth in one verse and lifting it up before the class like a diamond, to turn the truth this way and that, letting the sunshine of God's love shine upon it. The class sees one beautiful truth. The teacher puts it back in the "box," then brings out the next truth, turning it back and forth to reveal the "sparkles" of truth. Just so the teacher takes out each truth in turn, admonishing the members to practice this or that ideal in life. At the conclusion of the class the members are deeply inspired. Over the years I have gone through this experience in many Sunday School classes—and I have been inspired like the rest. But very few of these lessons ever led me to change my conduct. If our aim is conduct response, we need a better approach to developing the lesson.

Here is a second example of logical arrangement I copied from a teacher's quarterly published several years ago.

Lesson Title: Ruth, a Foreigner Who Found a Welcome.

Focal Passage: Ruth 2:8–13; 4:13,17.

Suggested Outline:

1. A Gracious Gentleman—2:8–9

2. A Grateful Stranger—2:10

3. A Generous Attitude—2:11–12

4. A Gentle Request—2:13

5. A Glorious Harvest—4:13,17

The quarterly gave the teacher additional lesson helps including comments, illustrations, and suggested subpoints. Ruth's story is certainly a beautiful incident in God's plan of the ages, and this is a beautiful outline.

But this beautiful outline is inappropriate for a conduct response lesson. Now let me give my evaluation of the logical approach as a possible way to develop the lesson when the teacher plans to use a conduct response lesson. *Topical arrangement (or logical arrangement) is absolutely the wrong approach to use with a conduct response aim.* The outline of Ruth makes a beautiful sermon. It dramatizes human need, possible romance, humility. It even has a good ending. However, the Sunday School lesson is not preaching, especially not when teaching a conduct response lesson.

We have already discussed the three purposes of a conduct response lesson:

▲ To understand the Scripture passage,

▲ To build Christian attitudes, and

▲ To commit to the new attitude.

The outline given above serves only one of those three purposes. It was also stated that in lesson development there were three questions the teacher should ask and answer. The above lesson plan suggests none of those questions or answers. It might serve admirably for a sermon or a devotional. But this lesson plan should not be used for developing a conduct response lesson!

Arrangement by Attitude

The attitude underlying the lesson aim should determine the arrangement when you teach with a conduct response aim. This could be called *psychological arrangement*. The teacher must keep two things in focus.

▲ Each of the three lesson aims (the conduct response aim, the inspiration aim, and the knowledge aim) requires its own type of lesson plan. This chapter focuses on the conduct response aim.

▲ The attitude is pivotal when you teach with a conduct response aim. That is why you should identify the attitude and write it down at the top of the section we are now discussing—Developing the Lesson.

How can you identify the attitude underlying the aim? Just think about your class members. Then ask yourself: "What points or insights will prompt them to think more clearly about this attitude? What will help them better commit themselves to this attitude?"

Once you have identified the attitude underlying the aim, examine the Scripture passage you are studying. What does the Scripture passage say about members' needs in light of your lesson aim? Once you have answered that question, you can arrange your lesson development according to the attitude you are trying to enhance.

This is arrangement by attitude, or psychological arrangement. The needs of the members in light of the attitude underlying the aim should determine what you will magnify, what you will use briefly, and what you will leave out. I have emphasized that not every truth in the Scripture passage can be used. The teacher will simply not have time in the total lesson plan to do this. By using a psychological arrangement the teacher seeks to build understanding and develop a deeper commitment to an attitude. Therefore the attitude underlying the conduct response aim determines what part (or parts) of the Scripture will be used and what will, of necessity, be left out.

How does this work in practice? After giving a brief overview of the entire passage, the teacher begins serious development of the lesson. She may focus on a verse or even a phrase within a verse. She may begin in the middle of the printed passage or at the end of the passage. That is, the teacher begins the serious development where the attitude underlying the aim begins or where it is emphasized. The teacher may even go to parts of the Bible not mentioned in the printed passage, but she does this to deepen class members' understanding and commitment.

An Illustration of Both Approaches

Few writers are able to write with such clarity that we understand exactly what they mean to say. Sometimes an example or illustration clarifies what a writer is trying to say. I have suggested that teachers develop their lessons by the psychological arrangement rather than logical arrangement. Below I compare the two arrangements by first outlining a lesson using logical arrangement, then outlining *the same lesson with the same Scripture passage* but using psychological arrangement. This logical arrangement was taken from an adult teacher's quarterly several years ago.

The Logical Arrangement

Lesson Title: The Church

Focal Passage: 1 Corinthians 12:12–13; Colossians 1:18–20; 1 Peter 2:4–9

Aim: To lead the class to join with Christ in building the church.

Securing Purposeful Bible Study:

Lesson Development:

Attitude:

(The teacher, most of the time in the logical arrangement, does not bother to write out the attitude underlying the aim. She has a general approach in mind. As to the arrangement of the content, the following is a *logical outline* of the lesson development. Get your Bible and read each verse of Scripture given with the outline and see how logically the lesson develops.)

Outline:

1. The Unity of the Church—1 Cor. 12:12–13

    (1) Unity in Multiplicity—1 Cor. 12:12

    (2) The Source of the Unity—1 Cor. 12:13

2. The Preeminence of Christ in the Church—Col. 1:18–20

    (1) Christ the Head of the Church—Col. 1:18

    (2) The Gift of the Father—Col. 1:19

    (3) Purchased at Great Price—Col. 1:20

3. The Rejected Stone—1 Pet. 2:4–8

    (1) Rejected by Man, Elected by God—1 Pet. 2:4

    (2) Built into a Spiritual House—1 Pet. 2:5

    (3) For the Believer, Joy; For the Unbeliever, Judgment—1 Pet. 2:6–8

4. God's Own People—1 Pet. 2:9

    (1) Elected by God—1 Pet. 2:9

    (2) Set Apart by God—1 Pet. 2:9

The Psychological Arrangement

Lesson Title: "The Church"

Focal Passages: 1 Corinthians 12:12–13; Colossians 1:18–20; 1 Pet. 2:4–9

Conduct Response Aim: To seek to lead the members to be on mission with God in the world this week:

▲ by giving a special witness to a fellow worker, or,

▲ by sharing old Adult Sunday School quarterlies with those in jail, or,

▲ by talking with a teenager who may be beginning to have a problem with drugs, or

▲ by visiting an elderly person in a nursing home.[1]

Lesson Development:

Attitude—Being on Mission in the World

1. What are some different ways we use the word *church?*

   (1) The church is beautiful (a building).

   (2) I am going to church at eleven A.M. (a worship service).

   (3) The Methodist Church has several million members (a denomination).

2. A Scriptural View of the Church—(a very brief survey of the Scripture passage)

   (1) Many parts, one body—1 Cor. 12:12–13

   (2) Christ is the Head—Col. 1:18–20

      A. Christ to be preeminent in all things—Col. 1:18

      B. Christ has reconciled us to Himself—Col. 1:20

   (3) We are called by God to be priests—1 Pet. 2:4–9

3. What does it mean to *be* the church?

---

1. See pages 139–140 in chapter 10 as to why the above aim with its multiple possible response aim does not violate the statement on page 49 in chapter 4 that the conduct response aim should be "brief enough to be remembered."

(1) A typical free-church definition. (Write definition on chalkboard.) "A church is a group of people of like doctrine who voluntarily band themselves together to promote the work of God around the world." What do you think of this definition?

(2) As you understand the church, is it a group who "voluntarily band themselves together" or is the church a group called into existence by God?

(3) What difference does it make?

(4) An illustration—Two pastors were talking. The first pastor said, "I'm pastor of a mission. I wish to goodness I could lead them to become a church." The second pastor said, "I'm pastor of a church. I wish to goodness I could lead them to become a mission."

A. What was each pastor saying?

B. Which one was more nearly correct in his point of view as you see it?

4. Brief glance at the ministry of Jesus. (Searching other parts of the Bible.)

Divide class into four buzz groups. Assign each group one of the four Gospels. Ask each group to find in their Gospel:

(1) Instances where Jesus was engaging in a ministry.

(2) What was He doing?

(3) Where was it being done? Let each group report. Write ministries on the chalkboard. (Note these are primarily in the world, not in the synagogue. Watch your time here.)

5. If the church is, in fact, the body of Christ:

(1) Where, then, must the church go?

(2) What must we (the church) do? (Translate the findings of the buzz groups into modern terms.)

6. What are some of the reasons the church doesn't do these things? Be as specific as possible in your response.

   (1) What are some of the problems we face in our own lives?

   (2) What would be needed to change them?

Remember that this is only lesson development. Some of these questions would have to be left out. We still have two major parts of the lesson plan—Making the Lesson Personal and Securing Carry-over. We will consider these in the next two chapters.

To Summarize

Teacher's Self-examination

Here are some questions teachers should ask themselves in considering the development of the lesson for a conduct response lesson.

▲ What attitude underlies the response desired?

▲ What is needed to give an understanding of the Scripture passage?

▲ What is needed to give understanding relative to this attitude?

▲ What questions will the members have that need to be faced and answered?

▲ What problems or difficulties relative to this attitude do the members have that need to be brought out in the open and considered?

▲ What will the teacher do to seek to deepen personal conviction in the area of this attitude?

Using Bible Content

I hope you can see clearly why the verse-by-verse method is the wrong approach in developing a conduct response lesson. Perhaps you are already devoting much of your class time trying to lead class members to a beginning understanding and a beginning conviction and commitment to an attitude. Even so, you still may get little, if any, specific response from your class members. The verse-by-verse approach is inspirational and enjoyable, but it simply does not lay the foundation for a response of changed lives that the teacher desires.

What method or methods should you use in developing the lesson? A variety of methods. But it is imperative that you get class members involved. In the outline of lesson development given above, the teacher divided the class into four buzz groups and had them search the Bible, give reports, and discuss. Certainly, the teacher also will share in the discussion.

The Teacher's Attitude

What I am calling the teacher's attitude refers to his total being, essential being, or spirit. If you are going to be a teacher who makes a difference in the lives of people, certain attitudes should characterize you as a person. These attitudes should be characteristic of your being all the time, but I mention them here in lesson development because these must be present in your life as well as in all your teaching, especially as you develop the lesson. Without them, little will happen.

Are you an open and honest person? In the total class setting, does the teacher demonstrate the spirit of an open and honest person? The teacher deeply desires that the class members, whatever their age group, will deal openly and honestly with the biblical truth being studied. This will not happen unless during the class session the teacher shares with the class his or her own struggles, problems, difficulties, or hang-ups in an open and honest way. If teachers do not lead the way and set the example, too many classes will deal with serious biblical truths in a shallow and superficial manner. This does not mean that the teacher should reveal the deepest doubts, problems, or difficulties of his life. Certainly we all have not only the right but the responsibility to keep certain parts of our life private. But it is the responsibility of the teacher to model openness and honesty for the class members to deal seriously with the biblical truth being studied.

Are you a caring person? The teacher also must develop a climate in which class members know that the teacher really cares for them. I once heard the pastor say to the congregation of which I was a member, "What happens to you makes a difference to me." This was certainly characteristic of his ministry, and I have never forgotten that statement. Nothing can take the place of this basic Christian attitude, and class members quickly sense its presence or its absence.

Are you a relational person? Through all of her relationships, the teacher must communicate: "You are important to me. I identify with you. I understand." Learning takes place in relationships. It is communal. In this relationship the teacher says: "I share with you my life. I expose myself to you and your possible daggers. I am willing to take this chance. Christ gave His life for you, and I give my life to you." The teacher can't fake this. The teacher can't do this unless she genuinely cares.

Are you a listening person? Many teachers tend to lecture. Some teachers resent the interruptions of class members with personal needs. These teachers need to be aware that what a class member says may be more important for his or her learning than what the teacher says.

Listening Can Be Dangerous

In listening we run the risk of hearing.
In hearing we run the risk of caring.
In caring we run the risk of becoming involved.
Listening can be dangerous.

Listening with our whole being is one of the most easily neglected aspects of communication. The teacher must do more than listen to words. The teacher must listen for what is behind and beyond another's words. There must be genuine, sensitive listening, and the teacher cannot (or will not) do this unless he genuinely cares for each member.

8

Making the Lesson Personal

A Difficult Task
    General and Specific Approaches
    Reasons Why the Specific Approach Is Better

Six Problems of Unguided Application
    Meaning
    Relationship
    Prejudice
    Information
    Personal and Social Pressures
    Complex Situations

The Life-Situation Technique

Three Principles for Using Life Situations
    Be Realistic
    Offer Two Courses of Action
    Apply to the Lesson

Mistakes to Avoid

Variations

Mrs. Hopewell had just finished teaching the Sunday School lesson to her class of adolescent girls. She was rather pleased with her lesson that morning. The theme was "God's Love for All People." She had brought out the fact that God loves everyone regardless of how rich or how poor they are. She had pointed out that Christians should show love to all people. The girls had entered vigorously into the discussion and all indicated their commitment to this Christian ideal.

On her way into the worship service, Mrs. Hopewell passed some of her girls and saw them whispering together, laughing at another girl because of the cheap dress she wore. Her heart sank. The girls had not learned the lesson after all!

Mrs. Hopewell's problem is the same as that which all Christian teachers face: how to get those whom we teach to apply the Christian ideal discussed in class to specific situations in their daily lives. In this chapter we focus on the fourth step of the conduct response lesson plan—how to make the lesson personal.

A Difficult Task

It is not so difficult to cover a portion of Bible material, or to explain a spiritual truth, or even to teach Bible knowledge; but when the teacher tries to instill spiritual truth into the lives of class members, he or she undertakes a difficult task.

General and Specific Approaches

To get the spiritual truths of the Bible into the lives of people is the ultimate objective of all Sunday School teaching. In meeting this objective, there are two approaches that may be followed.

By and large, Sunday School teachers have followed the more general approach. That is, the general spiritual truth is presented and explained, the application is made, and the class is exhorted by the teacher to follow the spiritual truth.

For example, during a study of one of the Gospels, the teacher may have a lesson on "The Sacrificial Christian Life." In developing the lesson the teacher may point out instances in the ministries of Jesus and the disciples in which they had made personal sacrifices. The teacher could draw some generalized conclusions, and then exhort the class to go out and live a sacrificial life.

In the other approach, at this point in the lesson plan, the teacher must have a more specific aim in mind, leading the class members to ask, "What specifically should I begin doing that I am not now doing to demonstrate my union with Christ in His sacrificial life?" The teacher leads the class to identify and face specific situations in which they are falling short of the Christian ideal. Only in this way will changes in life and action take place.

Reasons Why the Specific Approach Is Better

A fair and frank analysis of this generalized approach reveals that it has not been as successful in securing results in Christian living as might be desired. The general approach seems to be based on the assumption that if a person knows what is right or knows a spiritual truth, he or she will practice it. Therefore, the teacher conceives his or her task as bringing out all the truths in the lesson so that members will *know* them, with the hope that they will *practice* them.

One day a salesman was putting pressure on a certain farmer, telling how much a set of encyclopedias would help him. He told of all the information in the books that dealt with farming and pointed out how this information could improve the farmer's crops. Without a word, the old farmer listened to the sales talk. Finally, he stroked his beard and said, "Now listen, friend, this set of books you are selling may be able to teach me many things I don't know about farming. But I want to tell you this; I already know a whole lot more about farming than I'm using."

In too many instances those of us who claim to be Christian are like the farmer. While it is true that our knowledge of the Bible is exceedingly limited, it is even more true that we know a lot more about the Christian faith than we are using. We know more about evangelism, forgiveness, and loving, Christian living than we are practicing.

We must conclude that simply to know a spiritual truth does not necessarily mean it will be followed. Therefore, we must not rely solely on a general presentation of spiritual truths to the class members to get desired results.

The mind-set of class members is often against making a change in their way of living. While there are many exceptions to this statement, one wonders whether this attitude is not more prevalent than we care to admit. To what extent do people come to Sunday School with the attitude that all that is necessary is to come, sit, agree with what is said, and leave? They all agree in general with the spiritual truth that is presented, but they do not plan to do anything specifically about what is taught and go right on living as they have been living.

Two factors have unconsciously hindered my learning in Sunday School. These are what I call the then-and-now factor and the them-and-us factor. As I grew up in Sunday School as a youth, and even as an adult, somehow I felt the things I was studying in the Bible (especially in the Old Testament) happened "way back then." Somehow it must have been easier to do right then than now. "Back then," they heard God talk. Some of them even walked with God. I felt if I had lived back in Old Testament times, I could have been holy. But now things were real and therefore different. Did the things that happened in the Bible really happen on this planet? Somehow, I never identified the Bible world with my world. Then-and-now was difficult for me.

But so was them-and-us. I felt it must have been relatively easy for Isaiah, Amos, Peter, and Paul to do the things they did. Isaiah had a vision. Peter saw the resurrected Christ. Paul had that phenomenal conversion experience. If I could have a vision, or see the risen Christ, surely it would change my life too! But nothing ever happens to me, and I am skeptical when I read that other people have visions. I'm just a real person living in this time and place with all of the everyday problems. I can understand why there are all sorts of games people play to avoid meeting God in real encounters. We really are "God-evaders." I can understand if, at times, the events of the Bible and the characters of the Bible do not seem real to us.

Can it be that we teachers and preachers really do not expect our members to do anything definite with what we teach and preach? Is it our fault that people have developed the attitude that all that is necessary is to come, sit, listen, and agree with what is said? If this attitude exists at all, it must be changed before we can get the results in Christian living we desire.

Six Problems of Unguided Application

It is exceedingly unwise for the teacher to leave it to the class member to make his or her own unguided application. Yet, in the final analysis, members must make their own decisions if they are to be meaningful and experiential. *Unguided* is the key word in the above statement. There are teachers who say, "I simply teach the Bible and leave it to my class members to decide what they want to do about it." Such a procedure is not a valid one to follow in securing changes in the lives of people. Consider some of the problems involved.

The Problem of Meaning

Often the class member may not know the meaning or significance of the teaching of Jesus for his or her personal life. For example, in the Sermon on the Mount, Jesus said, "Blessed are the poor in spirit." If the class member attempted to carry out this injunction of Jesus, what would he or she start doing next week, specifically, that he or she has not been doing? The average class member would find it exceedingly difficult to think of a definite conduct response that would fulfill this teaching of Jesus. (Try to think of one yourself.) As a result, most members, if left to make their own unguided application, would probably make no application at all.

It is not easy to translate the spiritual truths of the Bible into specific conduct responses for daily life. For that reason, the teacher must not wholly rely upon teaching generalized truths.

A religious educator once told of an experience a pastor had with some children of his church during a class session. He had talked to them about the Bible verse, "Be of good cheer, I have overcome the world." During the discussion the pastor asked the children, "What does this verse of Scripture mean for your personal lives?" The children did not know. He said to them, "It means that in your normal experiences you are to be cheerful in spite of difficulties and hardships." The minister then asked the children to give examples in their daily lives in which this principle could be applied. They could think of none. These children had accepted the teachings of Jesus, but they needed guidance to know how this particular teaching would operate in their daily conduct. Some may contend that surely adults ought to be intelligent enough to make applications of Jesus' teachings in their specific life situations, but even for adults it is not easy.

The Problem of Relationship

An individual may not see the relation between a particular life situation in which he or she finds himself or herself and any spiritual teaching. For example, when a person has suffered a gross injustice at the hands of another, he or she may not think of the biblical injunction, "Turn the other cheek." Or when an individual comes to vote, he may vote on the basis of party loyalty or prejudice and never think of his spiritual ideals. When a person rides through the slum area of a city or through a poor section in the country, he or she may never think of relating recently taught spiritual teachings to these social ills. For this reason, the person needs guidance in lifting these specific instances to the level of consciousness. Then the Holy Spirit might convict the learner for a lack of concern and inactivity in these and other areas. Under that conviction, the individual may be led to Christian activity and to a higher realm of Christian living.

The Problem of Prejudice

Prejudice sometimes makes one unwilling to apply Christian ideals. In the lives of too many of us, prejudice rather than spiritual truth plays the dominant role in determining our conduct. When prejudice and spiritual truth come in conflict, people often hold spiritual truths in their minds while their lives are guided by prejudice. Christian people accept the ideal that "God is no respecter of persons." But when this spiritual ideal is made specific to the treatment of minority groups, far too many Christians deny the spiritual truth in practice and are governed by prejudice. People must be led to evaluate their prejudices in specific situations if a change in attitude and conduct is to be secured.

The Problem of Information

Often an individual has insufficient information to understand how the Christian ideal would operate in many of the normal relationships of life. Persons may think they are acting as Christians when in reality they are merely living up to the current social standard which may be, and probably is, less than Christian. Consider an individual in business unaware that he or she is unchristian in certain business practices and activities because he or she is not aware that the prevailing business code is unchristian in these areas. Change will not come in an individual's life until such areas are specifically brought to the person's understanding.

The Problem of Personal and Social Pressures

Individuals may be unable or unwilling to make personal, specific application because of pressures from society or pressures they place on their own lives. Being human, we are all subject to the weakness of the flesh. In the conflict between the flesh and the Spirit, the individual needs to be helped and guided. For example, when an individual has caught a vision of the high road of the Christian life, there is a deep urge to live that high life. But as the individual looks around, he or she sees few who are traveling that road; indeed, most church members are traveling a lower road. Therefore, because of difficulties involved in traveling the higher road and because of weakness within oneself, the individual turns from the high road to walk the lower one with the rest of the people.[1] One tragedy of modern Christianity is that we have become so accustomed to traveling this lower road we have identified it as being the norm of Christian living. We are all aware of the weaknesses of the flesh and the temptation to rationalize our actions to keep from facing the difficulties and the challenge of traveling the higher road.

Take, for example, a man who becomes keenly conscious of some glaring sin in his community. He wants to take his religion seriously and fight that sin. But he knows that if he does, he will stick out like a sore thumb. People, even church people, will say, "He's fanatical," or "He's crazy." No one wants to be considered peculiar, and so the man decides that, since no one else is doing anything about it, he will not either.

Consider a teenage girl who, like every other teenage girl, wants to date. Night after night she sits by the telephone waiting for it to ring. She knows what is right and what is wrong. In general, she wants to do what is right. Yet the desire to be popular and get a date is so great she begins to relax her moral standards. People in situations such as these do not need to be left alone to make their own applications. They need to be helped, strengthened, guided, and supported.

The Problem of Complex Situations

Often, there is no clear distinction between right and wrong in many of the complex situations of life. The Christian does not face much difficulty in making decisions when the issues involved are either definitely right or wrong. But the Christian does have difficulty in making decisions when the issues are unclear. There are people who say a person who really is a Chris-

---

1. See M. Scott Peck, *The Road Less Traveled* (New York: Simon & Schuster, 1978).

tian will be able to tell the difference between right and wrong. This is not as simple as it might seem on the surface. For example, a rather large group of preachers was asked the question, "Was it right or was it wrong to drop the atomic bomb on Hiroshima?" About 50 percent of them said it was right; the others said it was wrong. The fact that they were Christians did not give them automatic insight or agreement about basic morality in this situation.

Young people particularly are always plaguing their teachers with the question, "Is it wrong to . . . ?" It is not the task of the teacher to tell individuals dogmatically what is right or wrong. It is the teacher's responsibility to lead a thorough, systematic study of the question under consideration so that individuals and groups may determine for themselves the Christian attitude or the Christian course of action. After all the facts have been secured, after all the information has been brought to light, after the group has discussed the different viewpoints, the group may be led to decide, individually, what is Christian in this particular matter. Of course, it is entirely possible—perhaps probable—that there will continue to be differences of opinion within the group. But, at least, each one in it will come to his or her own decision on the basis of information and inspiration that was not available before such a study was made.

The teacher is not merely a disinterested member of the group while this study is taking place. The teacher is a responsible member of the group, making his or her own contributions and giving guidance to the whole teaching situation. Naturally, it will be the teacher's desire that all decisions will be made with intelligence under the guidance of the Holy Spirit. Because the class members are going to make decisions one way or the other, the teacher must give more attention to helping them solve the specific problems they face as they seek to discover for themselves what is Christian.

The conclusion seems inescapable that teachers must become more specific in their teaching. Generalized teaching is the basic reason for the teacher's failure to secure more carryover from teaching. If we are going to teach for results, we must make the teaching personal. The assumption that the teacher can teach general principles and leave the class members entirely unguided to make their own specific application seems not to be a valid or safe assumption. There are too many things against the learner making these applications, especially when it would involve change in his or her life.

By way of analysis, what might happen within the learner who is left to make his or her own unguided application? First, the learner may make a valid application and follow it. What has been said thus far is not to be interpreted as meaning that Sunday School teaching as it is now being done is a failure. There are those who take teaching seriously, who earnestly undertake to find and follow the will of God, and who make intelligent application of teaching. We ought to thank God for these.

The second response is perhaps more prevalent than the first. The learner hears a certain teaching and applies it to the areas in which he or she is already following it but fails to apply it in other areas. For example, if the lesson is on honesty, an individual may call to mind all of the areas in which he or she is completely honest, but the probability is that the individual will not think of many areas in which he or she is not honest. A third reaction is the individual who does think of some areas in which he or she is not practicing a certain teaching; the likelihood is that the individual will rationalize his or her position and remain of the same mind.

Thus the teacher must recognize the fact that it is difficult to secure change. People resist it, particularly when it involves change in attitude or change in personal conduct. Therefore, if teachers are to secure conduct response and action from their teaching, they will have to use something more than generalized teaching and general exhortation to accomplish these desired ends.

The Life-Situation Technique

The teacher may make the lesson personal through the use of a life situation or, as it may be called, a "what-would-you-do?" situation.

How does this fit into the lesson plan? First, the teacher has introduced the lesson and secured a purposeful study of the Bible. Second, the teacher has developed the lesson. During this development of the lesson, through study of the Scripture, questions, and discussion, the members of the class have come to the point where there is general acceptance of the aim the teacher had in mind. Third, it is at this point in the lesson plan the teacher should use a life situation to make the teaching personal.

Suppose the teacher has a class of early adolescent boys and has as his aim: "To seek to lead my class members to tell the truth to their parents in spite of difficulties." In the development of the lesson the teacher has led the group in a study of several passages related to truth. They have studied John 1:14; John 8:32; and John 14:6. During the class several questions have been raised and some objections voiced. All but a couple of them come to a consensus that everyone ought to tell the truth all the time even though it is not easy to do. The following life situation might be used:

Jimmy came in from school and found a big piece of chocolate cake on the table. He proceeded to eat it. Later, he heard his mother go in the kitchen and then say in a loud voice, "Who ate that last piece of chocolate cake that I had saved for Mrs. Brown?"

Jimmy was scared. Just at that moment his sister, Mary, came in. She had been eating chocolate candy and had chocolate smudges all over her mouth.

Naturally, Jimmy's mother thought Mary had eaten the cake. Mary denied it, but her mother would not believe her. The mother said, "Mary, I know you ate that piece of cake and I am going to punish you for doing it!" Jimmy heard all of this from the next room. He kept perfectly quiet, but he was thinking hard. He knew if he kept quiet Mary would be punished. What would you do?

In leading the class to face this situation, the teacher leads them to consider the lesson aim of telling the truth to parents in spite of difficulties. This type of situation would also make the lesson real to the class. Earlier in the lesson most of the group may have agreed that all boys and girls ought to tell the truth to their parents. But when they are confronted with a life situation such as this, they will no longer answer glibly or consider the matter superficially. In a life situation, they see what the teacher is talking about and realize that they themselves might be involved in a similar situation.

Two things need to be called to the teacher's attention at this point. The first has to do with the question, "What would you do?" It is important for the teacher to ask the question exactly as it is given with a particular focus on the "you." Although in the life situation the teacher may have been telling about "Jimmy," or "Mary," or "Mark," or "Susan," the question to be asked is, "What would you do?" Using real names in the situation helps the class look at it from the outside, but "What would you do?" brings them into it at the end of the situation as the teacher desires to do. Second, although this is called a life situation, the situation does not necessarily have to be a true situation. It may be or may not be. It may simply be a hypothetical situation that comes from the imagination of the teacher. Or it may come from something the teacher has read in a newspaper or magazine. However, the teacher must know the members of the class so well that he will be able to make up situations so closely related to the normal experiences of the group that they are real to them; otherwise they will be of little or no value.

Look at another example. The teacher of a class of sixteen-year-old boys, having the same aim, might use this life situation:

> Tom is a senior in high school and has been driving the car by himself for about a year. One day Tom's dad called him in and said, "Tom, you know that you and I have always shot straight with one another. You also know that I have never tried to spy on you in order to catch you doing something. However, word has come to me that you have been driving the car rather fast and recklessly. Son, I want us to have an understanding. I am going to trust you to drive the car properly. I am not going to be a watchdog to see whether you do or not. I am going to trust you. However, if you ever get a traffic ticket for speeding, I will take away your privilege of using the car for three months. Is that fair, son?" Tom admitted that he had been driving the car too fast sometimes, and he agreed that what his dad proposed was fair and perfectly satisfactory with him.
>
> Some months passed. Tom had forgotten the conversation with his father. One night he and Jerry were double-dating with their best girl friends. They were having a wonderful time talking over plans for winning the prize at the scavenger hunt to be held soon. They were so excited with their plans that Tom forgot to watch the speedometer. Before long, a siren was heard behind them. A police officer handed Tom a ticket for speeding. It was then Tom recalled with a shock his conversation with his father. With downcast face Tom told his friends about it and said he would not be able to use the car for the scavenger hunt as they had planned. The group was keenly disappointed. Then Jerry said, "Tom, I have an idea. You give me the traffic ticket and I'll pay it for you. Your dad will never know anything about it." The girls enthusiastically agreed that this was the right solution. Tom hesitated. What would you do?

When this life situation was used in teaching the group of teen-age boys, one said, "I would wait until after the scavenger hunt and then tell Dad about it." His solution was an indication that he had failed to see the full implications of telling the truth. Real truthfulness for the Christian is a willingness to tell the truth regardless of the consequences, even if the individual knows that punishment will follow. Although the young man's response was an indication that the lesson had become realistic for him, it also indicated that the truth, though accepted, had not been fully learned.

Three Principles for Using Life Situations

Principle #1: Be Realistic

The life situation chosen must have the ring of realism for the class. For example, the teacher of an average group of adolescents would not use a situation in which someone had to determine what to do with a million dollars. Such a situation would not be realistic for this group. A situation in which a decision had to be made concerning how to use several extra dollars would be more appropriate.

The teacher should take care to work out a situation in which the members could easily be involved. It should be so realistic that the class would identify themselves with it and become emotionally involved in it. To achieve this, it must be realistic for them.

Principle #2: Offer Two Courses of Action

The life situation must present two courses of action. One is the human response. In following this course of action, the individual would be doing what comes naturally. For example, in the first life situation given earlier in this chapter, the natural thing for Jimmy to do would be to remain quiet and let his little sister get the punishment. In the second life situation, the natural course of action would be for Tommy not to tell his dad he had gotten the traffic ticket. In working up a life situation, it is important that the teacher put into it all of the pulls and tugs he can to make the human course of action the more desirable one to follow. That is the way life goes. The Christian course of action is the other alternative. Of course, in presenting the life situation, the teacher does not say that there are two ways open for the group to follow. But he takes care to see that the two possible courses of action are involved.

Principle #3: Apply to the Lesson

The life situation must be one in which the class will apply the teacher's lesson aim in making the proper choice. In the example of Jimmy and the cake, if he had chosen to confess that he had eaten the cake even though he knew his mother would have punished him, then he would have been fulfilling the aim of the lesson, which was "to tell the truth in spite of difficulty." The teacher does not reveal the lesson aim to the class, but it must be inherent in the situation.

Using a life situation is not the same as applying the lesson to life. In applying the lesson to life the teacher points out how the truths that have been discussed in the lesson would apply to life. She concludes with an exhortation to the class to follow them. A life situation makes no generalized application but presents the spiritual problem involved in the lesson in terms of a realistic, specific situation in which the members could easily be involved. It takes the spiritual truth out of the realm of the abstract or theoretical. This approach enables different age groups to see much more clearly the relation of a religious truth to life because it is presented in terms of a concrete life situation. A conflict is involved; a choice must be made.

A life situation is not the same thing as an illustration. An illustration is a story or incident that is complete in itself. In an illustration, the end or outcome is told. In a life situation, the end or outcome is not told. The group is led to the point at which a decision must be made, but the decision is not given. At the climax of the conflict, when the struggle between the human and the Christian response is at its peak, the teacher confronts the members with the question, "What would you do?" This is one of the values of a life situation: Since the outcome is not told, the way is opened for discussion of possible outcomes that may be suggested by the members of the class.

Teachers often use illustrations and think they are life situations. What is the difference between an illustration and a life situation? An illustration tells the class what someone did or said, or it describes a situation that happened. In a Sunday School setting it is designed to encourage the class to follow this example (or not to follow it as the case may be). In a life situation, the teacher tells of a realistic, conflict situation, raises it to the level where a difficult decision must be made, and then asks, "What would you do?"

If the class members do not respond when the teacher asks, "What would you do?" the teacher must lead the group to confront the issue until they do. He should give the class some time to think and then ask, "Well, what would you do?" They may not be sure what they would do. It may be that for the first time they are beginning to see how the spiritual truth can be operative in their daily experiences.

What should be done if the class members respond lightly? What if one of the members of the group gives the correct answer just because he knows it is the correct answer? The teacher will have to discern whether the answer is sincere. If the answer is given lightly, there are at least two things that the teacher might do. She might ask, "Is that what you really would do?" A few probing questions such as this will let the class members know the teacher is not satisfied with any light answer. Or, if the situation is so real the class has become emotionally involved, the other members will usually respond to the one who answered lightly with the proverbial, "Oh yeah!" Often the other members of the class can handle such a situation more effectively than the teacher can.

It is important that the teacher save ample time for this part of the lesson. If the problem is real to the group and the decision is difficult to make, it is likely that the teacher will have to lead the group in rethinking the spiritual truth which they had so glibly accepted before. As the group discusses the difficulties involved and the courses of action possible, they may be telling the teacher what they really think for the first time instead of what they think the teacher wants them to think. After seeing what the spiritual truth might mean in a specific life situation, it may be necessary for the teacher to lead the class to reaccept the aim the teacher has in mind.

Using a life situation is only one more or less dramatic way to make the lesson personal. There are simpler ways. For example, the teacher might say, "What does this lesson mean for your personal lives?" Or, the teacher might say to the class, "You give me a situation from your experience in which this spiritual truth we have been considering would be involved." Here again, variety is the spice of life.

Certainly, the teacher will not use a life situation every Sunday. Probably it should not be used over once a month. (In fact, it will be pointed out in the next chapter that the conduct response lesson generally should not be used more often than once a month.)

It will be up to the teacher to devise other ways of making the lesson personal so that class members will be led to relate the spiritual truth to their personal lives.

There may be occasions when the teacher has a life situation so realistic that will involve the class so deeply that he chooses to introduce the lesson with the life situation. He then uses the section of the lesson plan called lesson development to explore not only the printed passage but also to explore teachings from the whole Bible related to the problem. This would give the teacher and members more time for discussion.

Mistakes to Avoid

There are some common mistakes made in using life situations. Often the life situation lacks punch or climax. It must fascinate the group, drawing everyone so strongly into the situation that they identify themselves with the characters in the situation.

For the teacher to tell the life situation using the second person pronoun *you*, rather than giving the characters names, weakens it greatly. Use only names or the third person pronouns (he, she, it) in telling the situation. Do not begin a life situation by saying, "Suppose you and Mary were. . . ." Make the situation completely objective by avoiding the personal pronoun *you* until the final question, "What would you do?"

When the life situation is not sufficiently related to the aim of the lesson, there is a lack of unity. If the teacher's aim has to do with some phase of reverence, it would be of no value to have a life situation dealing with neatness. The teacher's aim must determine everything that goes into the lesson. The Bible study, the lesson development, the life situation—all must be related to it.

The life situation is weakened when the teacher suggests alternatives to the class. For example, after telling a life situation the teacher should not say, "Would you do this or would you do that?" It is better to omit the alternatives and leave the decision completely open without suggesting any possible course of action. The class may present some alternatives the teacher has not even considered. Suggesting alternatives limits the thinking of the class.

Sometimes the right answer to the life situation is too obvious. The decision is too easy. When this is the case, it is usually because the teacher had not put into the situation all the temptations and attractions, pulls and passions, that are in real life situations and that lead individuals to make the human choice. At other times, the situation is not sufficiently real to the group. These situations, if they are to be real, must center in the everyday interests of the group. The teacher should ask himself or herself the question, "Could this happen, or is this situation likely to happen, to any of the members of my class?"

Finally, in some instances, the situation is not sufficiently related to the age group. If a teacher has a group of adolescents, she would not use a life situation about sixty-year-old adults. It is not easy for a teacher to make his or her teaching personal. But unless this is done, the teachings of Jesus will not become the living and guiding force in daily life that they ought to be. The results are worthy of whatever efforts the teacher may have to expend.

Variations

Using a what-would-you-do situation is not the only way to make a lesson personal. Here also, doing the same thing every Sunday is probably the best way to assure dull lessons. Variety is the solution. Another closely related way to use the approach suggested in this chapter is to ask the members of the class to construct and then share a life situation. Since this book focuses on teaching adolescents, youth, and adults, only the youngest adolescents might have a problem with this. A small class could do this as a group. A larger class should be divided into smaller groups. Sometimes a member of the class will have faced a life situation which he or she can share with the class.

Although the teacher must be careful not to confuse the life situation with an illustration, an illustration is an excellent way to emphasize and help bring life to a desired moral quality or action.

Another dramatic way for the teacher to bring life to a moral or spiritual truth is to work up a situation and let members of the class role play the situation. We should use role playing more in teaching because it is powerful and effective. This may demand a bit more time and effort on the part of the teacher, but if it is well done it certainly brings interest, involvement, and life to the class.

This completes the fourth step in the conduct response lesson plan—how make the lesson personal. In the next chapter we come to the fifth and perhaps most important step in the conduct response lesson plan.

9

Securing Carry-over

Planning for Carry-over
    Choosing a New Course of Action
    Making an Action Plan

Letting Members Make Their Own Suggestions

The Teacher's Follow-up

An Example

Carry-over—The Key to Success

Types of Possible Responses
    Group Chooses the Same Thing
    Individuals Make the Same Choice
    Each Member Makes a Different Choice

Four Essentials for Conduct Response
    Willingness to Do Something
    Identifying and Considering What They Might Do
    Choosing One Thing They Will Do
    Making Any Plans Necessary to Carry Out the Response

Budgeting Your Time

Is This Too Personal?

In this chapter we come to the last of the five steps in the conduct response lesson plan. A teacher may say to me, "Like everybody else, I have to work for a living, and I have only a limited amount of time I can give to preparing a lesson each Sunday. Which of these five steps is the most important so I will know where to focus most of my energy?" If I were pinned down by a question like this I would answer as follows. There are two steps I would have to choose. I would select step one, "How to state an aim with specificity," and step five, "How to secure carry-over." However, having said that I would go on to say, if the teacher is serious about making a difference in the lives of those that he teaches, he will have to focus his energy on mastering *all five* of the steps. No one of the steps is optional.

Five Steps in the Conduct Response Lesson Plan

1. Stating the aim
2. Securing purposeful Bible study
3. Developing the lesson
4. Making the lesson personal
5. Securing carry-over

Now consider step 5. I have said that one of the problems we confront in teaching Sunday School is that the lesson does not sufficiently carry over into the lives of the class members. Probably one reason for this is the teacher does not make specific plans for carry-over to take place. In concluding the lesson, the teacher often makes some general application and exhorts the class to comply. Or, in some instances, the bell rings before the lesson is finished, and the teacher is forced to make some hurried, concluding comments before the class is dismissed. If the teacher expects to secure definite results from his or her teaching, something more than this is needed.

Planning for Carry-over

Teachers often fail to secure results because no plans were made for results to be obtained. The time to remedy this is when the lesson is being prepared. Securing carry-over should be as definite a part of the lesson plan as the development of the lesson or making the lesson personal. This involves two things: choosing a new course of action and then making an action plan.

Choosing a New Course of Action

Each member of the class must choose a new way of expressing a Christian ideal in daily living. This should be a new course of action—doing something he or she had not been doing to express the ideal just studied.

Making an Action Plan

Then each member must make a plan for carrying out the decision. Sometimes the class may choose to carry out a group action or project. For example, a class of young adults may decide to sponsor a recreation program for the young people in the church. Obviously the response will take place outside the classroom, but the decision for action and at least the initial plan for action must take place within the class session.

Therefore, in the teacher's lesson plan there must be a section headed "Securing Carry-over." As the teacher plans the lesson she will identify the conduct response(s) the class members might make and write these down in her lesson aim.[1] The different types of responses the members might make are discussed later in the chapter. As the teacher plans the lesson she will make a list of several possible conduct responses the class members might make to the teaching of this lesson. This will help the teacher make the teaching session much more alive and personal. Securing carry-over is difficult both for learners and for teachers. It is difficult for learners because we all resist making significant changes in our lives. It is difficult for teachers because they must be very careful they do not to put pressure on the learners to make a response. For the response to be truly experiential for learners, they must be free, under the leadership of the Holy Spirit, in making whatever response is or is not made. However, in Christian learning the teacher desires to go beyond words to experience. It is in carry-over where this either does or does not take place.

---

1. This does not violate the quality of the lesson aim that says it must be "brief enough to be remembered." See page 49 as a review.

Letting Members Make Their Own Suggestions

Securing carry-over is not the same thing as application of the lesson to life. In applying the lesson to life, the teacher usually gives a list of things the members can do to apply the spiritual truth to their lives. The teacher then exhorts the class to apply the lesson to their lives. While the teacher must make definite plans for carry-over, it is far better for the class members to make their own suggestions as to what they can and will do the following week.

How can a teacher accomplish this result? It must be remembered that action imposed by an outside authority (such as the teacher) probably will not be meaningful in the lives of members. For the decision or course of action to be meaningful to the individual, the individual must choose it for himself or herself. This is eminently true in the realm of moral attitudes or spiritual action.

This does not mean the teacher is therefore out of the picture in influencing the lives of the members. There are three things the teacher should remember. In the first place, the teacher planning the lesson may list a possible response for each member, *but it is entirely possible for each of the members of the class to choose a different response.* If the response chosen by the member fits his or her need, the teacher has been highly successful. In fact, the member's choice will be better than the one the teacher had listed in the lesson plan because it was chosen by the member.

In the second place, even though the teacher may make some suggestions as to possible responses for the members, *it is possible for the member to take the teacher's suggestion and the response still be self-chosen.* For example, a father may come home on a hot summer afternoon and say to his two sons, "Let's go swimming." If they reply enthusiastically, "Oh boy, let's do!" the father has not imposed his will on them. Their response is just as surely self-chosen as if they had made the suggestion themselves.

In the third place, *it is important that the response have meaning for the learner.* For that to occur, the learner must have insight into both the situation he confronts and the desired response in that situation. The learner must clearly see the issues involved in a given response. He must be made aware of the conflicting interests, desires, and passions within his or her own life. Jesus constantly sought to lead His followers to understand what following Him involved. "If any man would come after me," He said, adding in effect, "let him count the cost."

The learner must not respond on a superficial basis like trying to please a teacher. The learner must be led to face the situation frankly and, in light of the total commitment of his or her life to Jesus and of his or her accepted generalized ideals, to choose what seems to be the Christian response in this particular situation. There must be true individual choice with no external pressure exerted. The decision must come from deep within the learner if it is to be either Christian or lasting.

The Teacher's Follow-up

The teacher also needs to have some plan to find out whether the lives of the members are really being influenced by his or her teaching. Admittedly, this is not easy to do, but in too many instances teachers have no idea whether their teaching is making any significant difference in the lives of those whom they teach. Yet this is the reason they teach! Too often at the end of a class session they have only a vague hope that they are doing some good. If the teacher does expect growth in the lives of the members, this vague hope is not sufficient. The teacher must find out what is really happening in the lives of class members.

There are several different approaches the teacher may use in securing this information. If the class decides to attempt a group project, it is easy to get this information. The teacher can simply observe the class members at work during the project, noting those who are involved and those who are not, which ones demonstrate joy in the work, those who take leadership roles, and those who are helpers.

When class members decide to make individual responses, the ways to get this information become more difficult. Does this mean the teacher is doomed to teach without knowing whether his or her teaching is effective? The serious teacher would like to know whether his or her teaching is helping those taught take growth steps in their lives. But how can the teacher do this without giving the learners the impression the teacher is checking up on them?

This is where it is so very important for the teacher to have built close relationships with the learners. If the teacher and the learners have built these close relationships with one another, then it is possible for the teacher to secure this information without giving the impression of prying or snooping. Often with adolescents, if the teacher has developed a close relationship with them, then during the class session he might simply ask for a report on what they did during the week to carry out the decisions made in class the previous Sunday. Informally, before the class, the teacher will be able to make inquiries. Certainly outside of class the teacher will be able to get this information through individual, informal conversations with class members.

A plan for follow-up with adults is also needed to let the class members know the teacher really expects them to do something about what is taught on Sunday morning. Some class members have gotten into such a habit of agreeing with what the teacher says without making any definite response to the teaching that they do not realize the teacher really expects them to do something with their knowledge or insight. The understanding must be instilled in the minds of the class members that this teaching is for life and for action.

With adults the depth and quality of the relationships that have been built between the teacher and each member is even more crucial. If the relationship between the teacher and the learner is close enough, there are several things a teacher might do. During the week the teacher could call a member and in conversation about the class on Sunday might say, "I was deeply impressed with the seriousness of the discussion we had last Sunday and the response you indicated you were going to start doing this week. I know this was deeply meaningful to you. I have been praying for you by name every day this week, and I was wondering how it was coming along?" Or the teacher might ask, "Have you run into any difficulties?"

Here's another suggestion. On Sunday morning the teacher may have a sheet of paper to give each person who makes a decision to start doing something he or she had not been doing before, and ask them to write their decision on the sheet privately. The teacher then gives them an envelope in which to put the sheet and asks them to seal it and write their name and address on the envelope. The teacher then tells the group she will put a stamp on the envelope and mail it to them on Monday so they will get it on Wednesday to remind them of the decision each made.

This would do three things. One, it would be a reminder of the decision the member made. Two, it would give the teacher a reason for calling to see if the letter arrived. Three, during the call the teacher could inquire how things were going in terms of their decision. It would not be long before the members would look forward to a call from the teacher inquiring how things were going in terms of their responses. These calls will mean more work for the teacher. However, if results are to be achieved, a follow-up must be made. An interested teacher who is vitally concerned whether class members are growing as Christians is not willing to leave teaching or its results to chance.

An Example

Now let's visit a class of early adolescent boys. Every class member decides to do the same thing, so it will be easy to determine how each member responds. The teacher has written his lesson aim: "To seek to lead my class members to be regular in attendance at the morning preaching service for the next quarter." During the lesson he has led the group in a meaningful study of the Bible, and the boys have accepted in general the idea that Christian people should worship God regularly. After this, the teacher presents the class with a life situation to help them see something of the difficulty involved in regular church attendance. After further study and discussion, the group accepts the aim that people should worship God regularly in spite of difficulties. The teacher then comes to the carry-over.

TEACHER: Do any of you know what percentage of our class attended worship regularly last quarter?

RESPONSE: No.

TEACHER (writing on the blackboard): We had only 30 percent. How does that strike you?

RESPONSE: That's not so good.

TEACHER: No, that isn't so good. In light of our discussion today, what do you think our class percentage for attending worship ought to be next quarter?

RESPONSE: It ought to be 100 percent.

TEACHER: Certainly, that is the ideal. But be more realistic. What percent do you think we actually ought to try for this next quarter?

RESPONSE: Eighty-five percent.

RESPONSE: Sixty percent.

RESPONSE: Seventy-five percent.

TEACHER: I see we have different ideas concerning the matter.

One says he will be out of town one Sunday next quarter. Another says his family is having company coming from out of town, and he doesn't know whether the family will come to church that Sunday. After discussion, the class agrees on 75 percent.

TEACHER: Now what are we going to do to help ourselves reach this percentage? We haven't reached it in the past, so if we are going to reach it, we will have to do more work than we have been doing. Does anyone have any suggestions that will help us reach this goal?

RESPONSE: Let's all sit together at the preaching service this next quarter.

MOST OF THE CLASS: That would be great!

ONE IN THE CLASS: Naw. I'd rather sit with my girl friend!

TEACHER: What about inviting the teacher and the girl's class to sit with us next quarter?

CLASS: Yeah. That would be fun.

TEACHER: All right, I will contact the teacher of the girls' class and also your parents and ask them if that will be agreeable with them. Are there any other suggestion you may have?

RESPONSE: We might have a committee to telephone everybody in the class on Saturday and remind them to stay for church on Sunday.

TEACHER: That's a good suggestion. Who would you like to have on that committee?

RESPONSE: I think it is too much to ask one committee to call the members of the class for three whole months. Wouldn't it be better to have three committees and let them phone for only one month each?

TEACHER: That is an excellent idea. Then let's select three committees.

The discussion continues until definite and specific plans are made to secure the carry-over in the lives of the class members. It is easy for the teacher to note the regularity of attendance the next quarter. The teacher must be careful not to nag any members because of irregular attendance. This can create serious problems.

Carry-over—The Key to Success

This is the point at which the nail is driven in up to the head. This is where the class simply ends in talk or a decision is made to make some response. All of the rest of the lesson has been generalized discussion about what might or should be done. In this portion of the lesson, all members are led to consider *what they are going to do.* Therefore, this part of the lesson is so important that it is necessary for the teacher to save plenty of time for it. If the bell ends the class session before the conclusion is reached, it is likely the values of the entire lesson will be lost. This conclusion must be unhurried. It takes time for class members to think, to make decisions, to draw conclusions, and to make specific plans as to what they will do.

It may be that this matter of carry-over is *the most important and least used* of the entire lesson plan. Many teachers may have a specific objective. They may start with the interest of the group and lead to a purposeful study of the Bible. They may have an interesting development of the lesson and make an application of the biblical truth. But it is at this point they stop short and fail to secure the carry-over into life experience.

The teacher makes the application and then exhorts the class to practice it in a fashion similar to this: "Christ spent His life helping others, so let us help those in need." Or, "Jesus is our model. Let's try to follow His example." Or, "We are living in a sinful world. Let's try to make our world a better place in which to live." Then the class is dismissed with prayer and no specific plans are made through which the members may carry out the matter discussed in the lesson. As a result, the likelihood is that the members, having agreed with the generalized concept, will go out and do nothing.

In planning for carry-over, more often than not the teacher should have in mind responses which each member may choose as the carry-over. However, there will be times when the course of action decided on by the class will be a class project. If the plans for the project are too involved to be worked out fully in the class period, it may be the class will have a special meeting during the week to work out the details of the plan to be followed. Or, the class may appoint a committee to study the problem and report to the class the following Sunday.

A teacher of an adult class had as his aim, "To lead my class to take some specific steps to provide a more wholesome environment for the social life of our high school group." In teaching the lesson he pointed out some of the evils in the community which served as a source of temptation to young people. One of the class members replied that something ought to be done to provide a more positively Christian environment for the high school students. The teacher faced the class with the suggestion, and the class unanimously decided to undertake this as a class project.

This project was, of course, too involved to be worked out in the class period. The class decided to meet at the teacher's home on Tuesday night for discussion and planning. At this meeting, they considered such questions as: What will be our plan of attack on this problem? What facilities of a Christian nature are available to our young people? What facilities of a questionable nature are available to our young people? What facilities of a distinctly unchristian nature are available to our young people? Should we make a survey as to where and how our young people spend their leisure time? What committees do we need?

Questions were faced. Answers were sought. Other class members became involved when they found out the class was serious about doing something. Other meetings were held. The courses of action were decided upon and put into effect.

Planning sessions such as these will not simply end in talk or with a general exhortation—"Let's all try to help our young people"—but in action. It could well be that in carrying out a response of this type, the class members might learn more practical Christianity than they would learn from just listening to a teacher for a number of Sundays.

Types of Possible Responses

The types of possible responses that may be made by a class or an individual are as varied as life. A list might include the following.

Group Chooses the Same Thing

In the first type of response, all members choose to do the same thing and they choose to do it as a group. This is what we call a class project. This would be like the example given earlier in which an adolescent class chooses to attend the morning worship service more regularly one quarter and to sit together as a class. This type of response would be used least often by the teacher.

Individuals Make the Same Choice

In the second type of response, all members choose to do the same thing, but they express it as individuals. A youth class together decided they would deepen their experience in prayer, but the particular expression of deepening their prayer life would be done by each member in his or her own way.

Each Member Makes a Different Choice

In the third type of response, each member decides to do something different. The following response is an example: "To seek to make my home a more happy place by. . . ." Each member would choose what he or she would start doing (or do more often or less often) to make home a happier place. In this response all of the class members probably would not do the same thing. The likelihood is that each member would choose to do something different. However each one is seeking to make this Christian ideal more of a reality in his or her life.

As I see it this type of response has the greatest potential for the class member and would be the type of conduct response the teacher would seek most often! It is more specific and more personal for the class member in that each one is able to choose the life response that would make the biggest change he or she is ready to make in life or in the world.

This is important. As the lesson is being planned, in working out the lesson aim, the teacher will write out a possible conduct response for each member. Depending on the size of the class, this will mean the teacher will write down as many as six or more different responses as a part of the aim. This immediately comes in conflict with a pivotal point made in chapter 4. There I said a good aim should be brief enough to be remembered. With this many different conduct responses the aim is certainly not brief enough to be remembered. How can this conflict be resolved? It really is very simple. Each member will choose only *one* response he or she is to put into practice, and the member, if he or she is serious, will be able to remember that one response.

Why is it probable the teacher will have a different response for each member? We Christians are at many different levels in our development and expression of the various general ideals and attitudes of the Christian faith. Some members have grown more in certain areas of the Christian life and other members have grown more in other areas. Also the members in a typical class will have different settings and different opportunities for expressing the Christian ideal being studied.

To suggest that the teacher work out a possible conduct response for each member does not imply that the teacher will suggest during the teaching session the specific responses the members may do. Indeed, the teacher must be careful not to do this! Remember, the response of each class member must be self-chosen! It must also be freely chosen! However, the teacher must lead the members to understand that if they do make a decision to make a specific response they are to demonstrate an evidence of the truth in their lives beginning that week!

I like to think of these responses as *growth steps* for each individual class member. This leads me to suggest another weakness in what we call applying the lesson to life. The thrust of the teacher's lesson up to this point has been to lead the class to accept the Christian ideal being taught. The application generally is an exhortation to carry out the Christian ideal.

When I was a child we had a game we called "May I?" In this game we could take giant steps and baby steps. The application is what I would call seeking a "growth step" in Christian growth. The teacher wants to challange the members to make a significant response and so the teacher generally calls for the members to take a giant growth step. Now I am aware in my own life that I need a lot of giant growth steps. But as I look back over my life, I have not grown by taking giant growth steps. I have grown by taking a lot of baby steps. Hasn't that been your experience too? So, letting each member choose a baby step that he or she is willing to take seems to me to be the best way to get a conduct response.

Four Essentials for Conduct Response

When the teacher is planning to teach a conduct response lesson there are four factors that need to take place in the life of the member if conduct response is to become a reality.

Essential #1: Willingness to Do Something

When the teacher plans each step of the conduct response lesson plan, planning to guide the thinking and discussion of the class, praying all the time, there is one thing the teacher is seeking to do. The teacher is seeking to lead each member to meet

God at such a deep level that each member, in his or her inner being, will have a *willingness to do something* in the area of the Christian attitude being studied. For a conduct response lesson, the teacher, under the leadership of the Holy Spirit, is seeking to lead each member to have the inner conviction and the motivation to take a baby step of Christian growth.

When the teacher comes to this point in the class session, in the time it takes to blink one's eye the teacher must evaluate by the interest that has been shown and the quality of the discussion whether the majority of the class seems to have this willingness. *If not, the teacher should not go on and seek to push a response on the members.* This first factor is pivotal!

Essential #2: Identifying and Considering What They Might Do

If, in the judgment of the teacher, a majority of the members through their interest and discussion have indicated they do have this willingness at a significantly deep level, the teacher is ready to go to this second factor. Here the teacher will lead the members to identify what a person might do (or not do) as a practical expression of the Christian attitude being studied. The teacher must make sure a member does not suggest a response that is not specific. The question, "How does one express it?" is a good question for the teacher to use to make sure it is not too vague and general. At this point the class is simply listing some possibilities that might be done. Nothing has been said about whether one is going to do anything.

In class at the seminary, the students asked why it was necessary for the Sunday School teacher, in planning the lesson, to make a list of ways the Christian attitude might be expressed in life if the class members were going to make the list on Sunday. My response was the teacher needed to be ready with some suggestions to prime the pump if the members couldn't think of any.

Essential #3: Choosing One Thing They Will Do

Obviously, this is the key factor. Up to this point the class has just engaged in discussion. But now the individual has come to the time of decision. Again it must be emphasized that any decision a member makes must come from a deep inner conviction and commitment. The decision must be completely self-chosen.

There must be absolutely no pressure from the teacher or others in the class. At this point each individual must be alone with God when the decision is made—whichever way the decision may go.

Essential #4: Making Any Plans Necessary to Carry Out the Response

If the decision is a project, this will need some planning time in the class. If it is a personal baby step that has been chosen, it will still be important for the individual to have a brief time to consider how this change is going to take place.

This means the teacher must save enough time in the class period for these four factors to take place. It takes time to think and consider. It takes time to make a serious decision about changing the pattern of one's life, even though it is a baby step. If the bell rings before the decision is made or if the teacher has to rush the class through these factors, there will be a very unsatisfactory conclusion to the lesson results. Bibles are closed. Chairs are pushed back. The teacher will have another chance, but this opportunity is gone.

Budgeting Your Time

With this chapter we have finished explaining the five steps in the conduct response lesson plan. I have already mentioned that plenty of time must be saved for carry-over to take place. You may be asking, "How much time should a teacher give to each part of the lesson plan?" This depends on several factors. It depends on the amount of time taken in the department assembly. It depends on the time taken for class business and records. In the final analysis it depends on the amount of time the teacher has for teaching. Assuming the teacher will have thirty-five minutes for actual teaching time, the following is a suggestion as to the approximate time given to each part of the conduct response lesson plan. For teaching purposes there are only four steps. (Working out the aim is a part of the planning process; it does not take teaching time.)

▲ Securing Purposeful Bible Study—5 minutes

▲ Developing the Lesson—12 minutes

▲ Making the Lesson Personal—10 minutes

▲ Securing Carry-over—8 minutes

I struggled over the approximate time that each part of the lesson plan would take. I kept thinking of the time it would take to lead members to meet God in a deep way in some area of their lives and the struggles they would have in making the decision to start doing something they had not been doing; I'm not sure we have the time to do all that. But that's what we are called to do as teachers. And we are grateful we have the leadership and power of the Holy Spirit.

Is This Too Personal?

There are teachers who say, "I just teach the spiritual truth and let the class members make their own application because I don't know what their particular needs are." Such an admission on the part of the teacher is no justification for ineffective teaching nor does it invalidate the principle that is here being suggested. It is the responsibility of the teacher to know the individual class members well enough to know their particular needs.

Other teachers say, "I teach the general truth because my class members need different things. When I teach the truth in general terms, each member is free to make his or her own application." It is true that the class members will have needs that differ, but this simply indicates it is the teacher's responsibility to adapt the spiritual teaching according to the differing needs of each individual.

Another teacher may say, "I don't want to be too personal." This is a valid consideration on the part of the teacher that must be faced. When a teacher leads the group to analyze and evaluate their present experience in light of some spiritual ideal, the discussion undoubtedly is getting personal. The teacher may feel that this kind of teaching is too personal and that the class members will resent it.

Three things need to be said. First, it depends on the *attitude and spirit of the teacher* as to whether class members object to this kind of teaching. If the teacher has built up the proper relationship between himself or herself and class members, if he or she demonstrates a sympathetic attitude toward the problems and viewpoints of all the class members, and if the class members understand and appreciate the approach of the teacher, they will welcome rather than resent such teaching.

In the second place, the teacher must use *common sense* in this type of teaching. She must recognize where the members are in relation to a given Christian attitude and lead them baby step by baby step toward the ideal. It is relatively rare that a person takes a giant step.

In the third place, it must be admitted that *there are probably some individuals who would resent having Sunday School teaching become this personal.* They would rather come to a class where the Bible truth is taught and their lives are not bothered. There are people who will accept everything that Christianity teaches so long as it does not affect or change their way of living. But when Christianity makes demands that would necessitate change, they get their feelings hurt and stop coming to church. In answering this objection, the teacher must decide for himself or herself whether the task of teaching is to rock people to sleep or to seek to lead them to grow in the likeness of Christ.

10

The Teacher
Plans the Lesson

Preparing for Lesson Preparation
    Set Aside a Definite Time for Study
    Find a Definite Place for Study
    Obtain Study Materials
    Prepare Yourself

The Teacher Plans the Lesson

A Comprehensive Lesson Plan

A Simplified Lesson Plan

Can the Teacher Achieve More
    Than One Aim in a Lesson?

▲ ▲ ▲ ▲ ▲ ▲ ▲ ▲ ▲ ▲

How will teachers prepare the lesson they are to present to their class next Sunday? What plan will they use? There are as many different ways of planning a lesson as there are teachers, and no one plan is best. Two teachers may use two completely different plans, and both of them may be excellent. The lesson plan suggested here is one that is compatible with the thesis of this volume.

I fear that many teachers follow a rather haphazard approach in preparing their lesson. Some feel they can wait until Saturday night to begin preparing. They scan the material in the lesson helps, read the suggested Scripture passage, get the general idea of the lesson, and then try to teach from this slipshod preparation. It is no wonder we have obtained few results from our teaching. If teachers seriously desire to lead their class members to grow in the likeness of Christ, to express in their normal everyday experiences the ideals of the Christian faith, this haphazard, incidental, and unworthy approach to lesson preparation must cease. Effective teaching demands the most careful preparation.

Preparing for Lesson Preparation

Even before the teacher knows what the lesson for Sunday is, there are some very important and practical matters concerning the teacher's preparation that must be considered and settled. Have you considered these simple matters and have you settled them in a way you feel is pleasing to God?

Set Aside a Definite Time for Study

The study of next Sunday's lesson ought to begin early in the week. Some begin on Sunday afternoon, but certainly all teachers should begin preparation by Monday if they are to meet the particular needs of their class and make the lesson real, personal, and alive for them. To find an introduction to the lesson that will immediately capture the attention of the class, or to find the right illustration to drive home a point, or to work out a life situation to make the lesson personal for the group requires time.

Not only should the study begin early, but definite times should be allotted during the rest of the week for teachers to continue their study. Unless definite periods are set aside the teacher will find that other matters interfere and the time for study is pushed aside. Once time has been set, it should be kept as faithfully as one would keep an engagement with an important person. It should be a time when there is a minimum of noise and interruption. Whenever it is, it should be a time of meditation and concentrated study.

Find a Definite Place for Study

Many teachers have found it advantageous to have a definite place for study. If teachers have a place where they are quiet and alone, the place will develop an atmosphere that is conducive to meditation, prayer, and study. Another advantage to such an arrangement is the possibility of having all needed materials readily available. It is exasperating to be ready to study and then have to spend time trying to find the lesson quarterly. To remedy this, teachers can keep the Bible, lesson helps, commentaries, and other materials all in one place so they are available when needed.

Obtain Study Materials

The study materials necessary will be partially determined by how much the teacher can afford to purchase. As a minimum, the teacher should have a good modern translation of the Bible and the lesson helps supplied by the denomination. The teacher should also have a good one-volume commentary of the Bible, a Bible dictionary, a Bible atlas, and a concordance. (See materials suggested in the box on the following page.) Teachers should also have at their fingertips a sheet of paper for each member which contains information about and, if possible, a picture of each class member. As the lesson is being prepared, the teacher will refer frequently to this notebook or folder to discover the different interests of the class members as well as their different needs. To have this intimate knowledge of the members of the class is an absolute essential.

Prepare Yourself

As teachers begin their personal preparation, it is readily apparent that their own attitude is quite important. Since they cannot do their best when they are tired, worried, or distraught, they should, if possible, plan to study when they are rested. If the cares and worries of the day weigh heavily upon them, they can prepare their own heart with a few minutes of meditation and prayer.

Physical preparation is not the kind of preparation needed. In studying the lesson teachers must ask themselves questions such as these: What does this particular lesson mean to me? Have I had any experiences with Christ in this area? Do I have the kind of faith I am going to try to teach next Sunday? Have I had experiences in prayer sufficient to teach my class? Do I have the missionary zeal that I need? Am I the kind of Christian witness I should be? Basically, teaching is a sharing of experiences, and teachers cannot share that which they have not experienced. Class members of every age sense any sham and pretense. So the teachers must prepare their own lives if they would teach effectively.

A Teacher's Bible Study Library
From Broadman & Holman

Study Bibles

Disciple's Study Bible
Master Study Bible

Commentaries

H. Franklin Paschall and Herschel H. Hobbs, *The Teacher's Bible Commentary* (1 vol.)
Layman's Bible Book Commentary (24 small vols.)
New American Commentary (39 large vols.)

Bible Dictionaries

Holman Student Bible Dictionary
Holman Bible Dictionary

Concordance

NASB Concordance

Bible Atlases

Holman Concise Bible Atlas
Holman Book of Biblical Charts, Maps, and Reconstructions
Holman Bible Atlas

Other Study Tools

Holman Bible Handbook
Paul House, *Old Testament Survey*
Joe Blair, *Introducing the New Testament*

The Teacher Plans the Lesson

When teachers are ready to begin specific preparation for next Sunday's lesson, they should first read the entire Scripture passage suggested in the "larger lesson." After they get the general background out of which the lesson was selected, they are ready for more intensive study. They will want to read the passage in a good modern translation. This should be followed by a careful study of the interpretation and comments in a reliable commentary. Any unfamiliar names or places should be looked up in a Bible dictionary. Everything possible should be done to master both the content and the interpretation of the suggested Scripture passage. Then they should consider carefully the suggestions given in the lesson helps they have available.

Five Steps in Planning a Conduct Response Lesson

1. Select the type of aim.
2. Devise a plan to secure interest of the class.
3. Work out the development of the lesson.
4. Make the lesson personal.
5. Secure carry-over.

After familiarizing themselves with the truths in the Scripture, they should consult the information compiled about each class member and ask what each one needs most from this lesson. In light of the answers to this question the teacher then selects a conduct response lesson aim. (This is the only type of aim we have discussed up to this point.) Then the teacher is ready for the second step in the lesson plan, which is to devise the plan for securing the attention and interest of the class and leading them in a purposeful study of the Bible.

The third step in the lesson plan is to work out the development of the lesson. In working out the lesson development there are two things teachers must particularly keep in mind. First, they must remember that in this part of the lesson they want the class to accept the general ideal that underlies the aim for the lesson. To accomplish this, the teacher must include all the material time will allow to lead the members to this acceptance *and must leave out of the lesson* all those truths which are as interesting and as important but which do not contribute specifically to the acceptance of the aim.

Second, the teacher must keep in mind that the lesson development must be designed to meet the need of each individual in the class. Because each member is different, the need of each will be different. A question may have to be asked especially for Mary's benefit. An illustration may have to be told in order to meet Ellen's need. A problem may need to be discussed for Joan to see her particular problem. The question is, does the teacher know the members of the class intimately enough to know what their particular needs are?

In the fourth step of the lesson plan, the teacher tackles the problem of making the lesson personal so the class members will come to see how the spiritual truth they have been studying would operate in an actual life situation.

The fifth step in the lesson plan is where the teacher plans the most important part of the entire lesson—the conduct response for the lesson. This is where the teacher plans carry-over. Here is where the teacher must plan how to lead each member of the class to: (1) decide whether they are going to *do* something about the truth they have been discussing, and (2) if so, to *identify* specifically what each member is going to do. The teacher must exercise the greatest care in planning to secure carry-over, for with a conduct response aim the lesson must not end simply in talk if it is to be effective.

A Comprehensive Lesson Plan

Undoubtedly the discriminating teacher has already asked the question, "How do the principles suggested in the preceding chapters fit together into a definite lesson plan?" Perhaps it would be helpful to the reader if some of the main ideas that have been presented are now lifted out and put together in outline form so that they may be seen as a whole. In working out a conduct response lesson plan the following matters should be kept in mind.

I. GENERAL PREPARATION

1. The teacher's preparation of himself or herself, in mind and spirit.

(1) through Bible study.

(2) through prayer.

(3) through meditation—what has this truth (in the lesson to be taught) meant to me in my personal experience?

2. What am I to teach?

(1) Study carefully the suggested Scripture passage including the larger lesson.

(2) Use commentaries and other lesson helps.

3. Who am I to teach?

(1) General information concerning class members.

(2) Specific information concerning class members.

II. A LESSON PLAN

1. What is my aim for this quarter?

2. What is my aim for this unit?

3. What is my aim for this lesson?

(1) A good aim ought to be:

a. Brief enough to be remembered.
b. Clear enough to be written down.
c. Specific enough to be attainable.

(2) What kind of aim do I desire?

a. Do I desire a knowledge aim?
b. Do I desire an inspiration aim?
c. Do I desire a conduct response aim?

4. How shall I secure purposeful Bible study?

(1) How shall I capture the interest of the group at the beginning of the lesson?

(2) How shall I direct this interest toward a desire to read or study the Bible?

(3) How shall I seek to ensure that the reading of the Bible will be purposeful and meaningful?

(4) What questions shall I ask the class in order to direct their study as they read the Scripture?

(5) How shall I lead in the discussion of the questions after the Scripture has been read?

5. How shall I develop the lesson? Write out the attitude to be developed (such as "be more loving").

    (1) What suggested material shall I use?

    (2) What suggested material shall I have to leave out? (The aim the teacher has in mind will determine this.)

    (3) What other material that is not suggested shall I use?

    (4) How shall I organize this material so that it will be in harmony with the needs and interests of my class members?

    (5) What questions shall I ask?

    (6) What problems shall I pose for the class to solve?

    (7) What method or methods shall I use?

6. How shall I make this lesson personal?

    (1) How shall I lead the class to feel that this spiritual truth affects their lives today?

    (2) How shall I help them to see a life situation in which this spiritual truth would apply?

    (3) How shall I seek to lead them to the conviction that this truth is not only right but that they should follow it in practice?

7. How shall I secure carry-over?

    (1) How shall I seek to insure that what I teach will not die in the classroom?

       a. Carry-over must be planned for.

       b. Conclusions must be unhurried. Adequate time must be left for this part of the lesson.

       c. Class members must suggest ways for the carry-over to occur.

    (2) What specific plans for this carry-over should be made?

    (3) What plan do I have to test whether any carry-over occurred?

8. How shall I stimulate interest in the study of next Sunday's lesson?

A Simplified Lesson Plan

The comprehensive lesson plan is far too complex and cumbersome for a teacher to use each week. The following then is given as a simplified lesson plan. The teacher can easily keep this in mind as the lesson is being prepared.

I. LESSON PLAN FOR CONDUCT RESPONSE AIM

1. Aim for quarter:

2. Aim for unit:

3. Lesson aim:

4. Securing purposeful Bible study:

   (1) To secure interest:

   (2) Transition:

   (3) What to look for or to note as Bible is read:

5. Developing the lesson: Identify attitude (Use only that material which will contribute to the achievement of your aim.)

6. Making the lesson personal:

7. Securing carry-over (be specific; lead to definite plans):

This lesson plan may be reproduced for teachers to use in their departmental group study in the weekly workers meetings or in their private study. If it is reproduced on legal size paper the teachers will have sufficient space to make detailed notes.

Can the Teacher Achieve
More Than One Aim in a Lesson?

In an earlier chapter I stated that it is unwise for a teacher to have an inspiration, knowledge, and conduct response aim in the same lesson. I also promised to point out why that was true. If the teacher has become aware of the vast amount of time necessary to lead class members to the point where they understand the relation of a spiritual truth to their personal lives and then are led to the point where they are willing to practice that spiritual truth, the teacher will understand that there is certainly not enough time in one lesson period to do more than secure a conduct response. Of course, in securing a conduct response a certain amount of knowledge is taught, but it is knowledge that will lead class members to accept and follow the spiritual truth under consideration. It is not a systematic study of a Bible passage necessary to lead the individual to have a comprehensive knowledge of some portion of the Bible. This will become even clearer for teachers after they read part 3.

The teacher will also face the fact that when she spends some time leading the class to master a significant portion of Bible knowledge, she will not have enough time to secure a conduct response. What has happened too often in the past is that the teacher has tried to accomplish all three of these aims in one lesson; and, as a result, none of them was fully achieved. The approach the teacher has to follow in teaching Bible knowledge and the approach to be followed in securing conduct response are so different that they cannot be adequately accomplished in the same lesson.

Therefore, my conclusion is that teachers must face the fact that if they are going to secure results either in the realm of Bible knowledge or of conduct response, they must determine ahead of time which aim they desire and stick to that one with singleness of purpose. Only in this way can definite, concrete, observable, and measurable results be obtained. With the next chapter we begin an emphasis on teaching with a knowledge aim.

Part III

Teaching with a Knowledge Aim

11. The Problem of Bible Knowledge

12. Improving Bible Knowledge

13. An Example of a
Knowledge Aim Lesson

14. Factors Related to
Teaching Knowledge

▲▲▲▲▲▲▲▲▲▲▲

11

The Problem of
Bible Knowledge

The Miller Survey (1932)

The *Pageant* Survey (1949)

The Bennett Survey (1959)
    Procedures
    Results

"The Bible and You" Test (1963)

The Gallup Surveys (1954 and 1982)

Barna Research Group (1990)

Let me share with you some studies that illustrate the seriousness of the problem regarding Bible knowledge. These facts are the reason for the depth of my concern. I am aware that teaching people a serious knowledge of the Bible is not our ultimate goal in teaching. People can get to heaven without a head full of Bible knowledge. We thank the Lord for this. But if the Bible is the Book we say it is—the inspired Word of God, the Book that tells us about God and about life—then for us who make these claims not to have a serious knowledge of this Book is nothing short of tragic!

The Miller Survey (1932)

One of the first rigorous surveys of this kind was Minor C. Miller's Bible knowledge test of 18,500 students in the public high schools of Virginia. Miller reported in 1932 that of the 18,500 surveyed, 16,000 could not name three prophets of the Old Testament. Twelve thousand of this high school group could not name the four Gospels. Ten thousand could not name three disciples of Jesus.[1]

The *Pageant* Survey (1949)

Five years later *Pageant,* a popular magazine, conducted a nationwide survey of Bible knowledge among children. The average child scored 46 percent. Protestant children, however, scored only 35 percent. The parents of Protestant children might explain this discrepancy by pointing out that Catholic children were taught the Bible in their schools five days a week. However, they could not explain away the next finding: children who did not attend Sunday School made an average grade of 30.4 percent! They had absorbed this much religious information simply because they lived in our culture. It is a sad commentary indeed to find that Protestants scored only 4.6 percent higher than those who did not attend Sunday School at all. Further, of those tested, 73.4 percent did not know the name of the disciple who betrayed Jesus, and 70.7 percent did not know that Paul was the apostle to the Gentiles.[2]

---

1. Minor C. Miller, *The Lost Bible* (Strasburg, Va.: Shenandoah Publishing House, 1932), 137.

2. *Pageant,* December 1949, 20–26.

The Bennett Survey (1959)

Russell Bennett became concerned that Sunday School members had little serious Bible knowledge. Under my supervision, Bennett developed a research project on Bible knowledge.[3]

Procedures

Bennett used scientific principles to devise the most valid possible test of Bible knowledge. This required far more than just making up a list of questions. Bennett prepared two sets of preliminary test questions before he was able to devise his official set.

The first test consisted of 150 open-ended questions. For example, "Jesus was born in the town of _____." Half the questions came from the Old Testament and half from the New Testament. This test was then given in four Southern Baptist churches (no churches were used that would later be given the official test). There were two rural churches and two urban churches. Of the two urban churches, one was a congregation mostly in the middle-income bracket and one congregation was in the high-income bracket.

The second test consisted of one hundred questions taken from the returns from these four churches. It was made into a multiple choice test by using the two most often incorrectly given answers to each question along with the correct answer. In the example given above, if the incorrect answer most often given in the blank was "Jerusalem," this was made one of the options. If the second incorrect answer most often given in the blank was "Nazareth," this also was made one of the options. "Bethlehem," the correct answer, obviously was one of the options.

Again, half the questions came from the Old Testament and half from the New Testament. Also this test inquired about the age and sex of the person, the number of years he or she had attended Sunday School, and the regularity of attendance. This test was given in three Southern Baptist churches (none of these churches was given the official test). One hundred tests were returned and, using a formula, it was determined that the test

---

3. See Russell Bennett, "Measurement of Pupil Bible Knowledge in Selected Baptist Sunday Schools in Kentucky." Master's thesis, The Southern Baptist Theological Seminary, 1957. Bennett is now Director of Missions for the Long Run Baptist Association, Louisville, Kentucky.

was valid; that is, the test measured what it was supposed to measure.

Based upon the results of this second test Bennett devised a chart to show how many of the best papers marked each question correct and how many of the worst papers marked each corresponding question wrong. The best questions would be those which all the best papers marked correct and all the worst papers marked wrong. Using this approach, the author was able to select fifty valid multiple choice questions for the official (third) test.

Results

The official test was given in seventeen churches in and around Louisville, Kentucky, during the regular Sunday School hour. In my judgment, this was a plus factor for the test. My assumption is that those who are somewhat regular in attendance would tend to have a more serious knowledge of the Bible than those who are irregular in their attendance or those who rarely attend.

There were fifty multiple choice questions on the test, and there were 695 completed tests to study. Of the fifty questions, the average correct score was 16.57.[4] I began to share this information with Sunday School teachers when I held conferences. I would say to the teachers, "This score meant the whole group flunked! They would have had to get twenty-five out of fifty even to make 50 percent! The fact is, they averaged only one out of three questions correct. Their average grade was only 33 percent!"

Then I would ask the teachers which age group they thought had the highest score.[5] Invariably, most responded, "Juniors!" with a few saying, "Intermediates." (These are today's older children and younger youth.) Laughingly, I would say, "Then you believe the longer one stays in Sunday School the less he or she knows about the Bible." The fact is, we do improve in our knowl-

---

4. The formula used in determining the score was: S=R-W/2. The score equals the number of right answers minus the number of wrong answers divided by two. This formula takes into account the factor of guessing.

5. Here I am using the age-group designations that were used in 1957, the year Bennett's study was done: Juniors (9–12), Intermediates (13–16), Young People (17–24), or Adults (25–up).

edge of the Bible as we grow older, but unfortunately it is a minimal improvement. Let me share with you Bennett's findings:

Age Groupings	Percentage Correct
Juniors (ages 9–12)	5.81
Intermediates (ages 13–16)	12.64
Young People (ages 17–24)	16.39
Adults (ages 25–up).	20.66

There was a mitigating circumstance in the unusually low score for Juniors (in addition to the fact that most teachers of this age grouping are far more concerned with helping children live according to the Bible than with teaching knowledge), and that is the knowledge test covered the entire Bible, both the Old and New Testaments. At these ages, they had not covered the Old and New Testaments with the depth they would as they grow older.

Here are two questions from the survey. These will give you an idea of the type and difficulty of the questions.

QUESTION: Jesus said, "He that would be greatest among you shall be:

_____(1) poor

_____(2) pure in heart

_____(3) servant of all

This question was missed by 64 percent of all who took the test.

QUESTION: The one who preached on the day of Pentecost was:

_____(1) Peter

_____(2) Paul

_____(3) John

This question was missed by 63 percent of all who took the test.[6]

Of course I did not want to rely too heavily on the results of one test. Bennett's test was carefully and scientifically con-

---

6. To check your memory, the answer to the first question is servant of all, and the answer to the second question is Peter. See Mark 9:36 and Acts 2:1, 14–40, KJV.

structed, but it sampled only a few churches in a small region. So I began testing other groups to confirm or question Bennett's results. I led a week of conferences at an encampment for Sunday School teachers and leaders during the summer of 1958. I also administered Bennett's test to the youth at the conference. Of course, I expected these young people to score much higher than the score from Bennett's group because their parents were Sunday School workers who took their vacations to come to this religious encampment. These youth were being brought up in the very best religious environment. Of the fifty-seven participants, the average correct score was 14.84. (The score for Bennett's group of young people was 16.39.) I could not believe it. I certainly have no explanation for it.

In those days I was leading conferences for Sunday School teachers almost every weekend. Naturally I shared the results of these two tests. This sparked a lot of interest and conversation among teachers. There was some disbelief and many questions.

"The Bible and You" Test (1963)

Shortly after, the Baptist Sunday School Board devised a Bible knowledge test entitled, "The Bible and You." Research and statistics specialists used the best scientific procedures in devising the questions and in giving the test. The test consisted of thirty-four questions, seventeen from the Old Testament and seventeen from the New.

This test was given in churches across the United States carefully selected to guarantee variety of location, education, and income. The project began in 1961. Its report, which was published in 1963, began with these words:

> The factual knowledge of Southern Baptists, or any other group, defies comprehension and accurate measurement. No area of such depth and breadth can be completely defined, let alone exhaustively plumbed. On the other hand, within carefully imposed and practical limits, soundings and measurements may be taken. The project herein reported was planned and conducted to provide a plausible, reliable, and valid indication to the current level of factual Bible-knowledge of persons, aged thirteen and above, who attend Southern Baptist Sunday Schools.[7]

---

7. *A Study of Factual Bible-Knowledge on the Part of Southern Baptists* (Nashville: Baptist Sunday School Board, 1963).

This test gave specific scores only for persons thirteen and older. Here are the number of correct answers (out of thirty-four questions) by age group:

Age Groupings	Number Correct
12 years and under	9.4
13–14 years of age	10.4
15–16 years of age	12.0
17–20 years of age	12.4
21–24 years of age	13.9
25–30 years of age	13.5
31–34 years of age	15.0
35–39 years of age	15.7
40–44 years of age	15.9
45–49 years of age	16.1
50–54 years of age	17.4
55 years and over	19.0

Now let's see how findings of "The Bible and You" compare with Bennett's findings. Let's compare the percentage of correct answers to the two tests:

	Ages 9–12	Ages 13–16	Ages 17–25	Ages 26–up
Bennett's Test	11.6%	25.3%	32.8%	41.3%
The Bible and You	27.6%	32.9%	38.7%	47.3%

In every age group, "The Bible and You" had a higher score than the group in Bennett's test. In the nine to twelve age group, it had a considerably higher percentage. As you see, however, no age grouping in either test ever reached 50 percent. And both tests reveal Southern Baptists' dismal lack of Bible knowledge, even among those who are rather regular in attendance in Sunday School!

How much does Bible knowledge increase as years go by? "The Bible and You" found some interesting facts. After studying the Bible from age seventeen through age twenty-four, youth increased in their knowledge of the Bible less than 1.5 percent. During the five years from twenty-five to thirty, Bible knowledge actually went down! For the fourteen years between thirty-one and forty-four those tested increased in their knowledge of the

Bible less than one point! Most amazing to me was this: The average group who were rather regular in Sunday School attendance had to be fifty to fifty-four years old before they could get *half* of the answers correct (seventeen out of thirty-four)!

Let me state again that I am aware that teaching or learning factual Bible knowledge is not the *major* purpose of teachers in our Sunday Schools. However, when we consider the amount of money a church spends building educational space and purchasing literature for Bible study; when we consider the amount of time people give in visitation; when we consider the amount of time teachers invest in preparing to teach the Bible; when we consider the time and energy pastors and church leaders give to promoting the importance of Bible study; for those of us who attend fairly regularly to have the weak factual knowledge of the Bible that these two tests indicate ought to cause the deepest concern among us and motivate us to rise up and do something about it!

Teaching factual Bible knowledge is not the major purpose for the Sunday School teacher, but it is a *worthy* purpose. And at certain times teaching for factual knowledge should be the major purpose of the teacher!

The Gallup Surveys (1954 and 1982)

This ignorance of the Bible is not peculiar to Southern Baptists. George Gallup Jr. and Jim Castelli, in a recent book, speak of the 1950s as a "decade of religious revival." However, they say,

> The state of religious knowledge in this period (as in later decades) was anything but impressive. Fewer than half the respondents in a 1950 survey could give the names of any of the first four books of the New Testament. And only one person in three could name all four books of the gospels. This sad state of biblical knowledge was also apparent in surveys taken in 1954 and 1982. When asked who delivered the Sermon on the Mount, 34% in 1954 and 42% in 1982 responded correctly. In 1954 only 35% of respondents could name the four gospels, but this increased to 46% in 1982. Where was Jesus born? In 1954, 75% responded correctly, but in 1982 only 70% knew. On two of these three questions, scores increased during this period.[8]

---

8. George Gallup Jr. and Jim Castelli, *The People's Religion: American Faith in the 90's* (New York: Macmillan, 1989), 8, 18.

Gallup and Castelli explain, "The level of religious knowledge increased slightly in the 1980s, but that increase was not particularly impressive given the vast increase in the proportion of college-educated Americans between 1954 and 1982, and the fact that a majority of Americans had attended Sunday school."[9]

Barna Research Group (1990)

More recently the Barna Research Group found that 93 percent of American households have a Bible, but 58 percent "do not know who preached the Sermon on the Mount" and 29 percent were "unable to correctly say how many apostles Jesus had."[10]

All of this research points us to the same conclusion. Even church people are seriously deficient in Bible knowledge. This is a serious problem that Sunday School teachers must face.

---

9. Ibid., 17.
10. Barna Research Group, *The Church Today: Insightful Statistics and Commentary* (Glendale, Calif.: Barna Research Group, 1990), 29-30.

12

Improving
Bible Knowledge

Definition of a Knowledge Aim
    Serious
    Systematic
    Significant
    Understanding
    Mastery

Lesson Plan for a Knowledge Aim Lesson
    Aim for Quarter
    Aim for Unit
    Aim for Lesson
    Begin with Interest
    Overview
    Organization of Material
    Summary and Review
    Assignment and Project

I have listed three lesson aims: the inspiration aim, the knowledge aim, and the conduct response aim. My strongest emphasis in this book has been on conduct response. Christians should be especially concerned about changes or growth in life when the Bible is taught or studied. However, I am also aware of tragic ignorance of the Bible, even among Christians.

When I shared this concern in a conference, a teacher said this was not true in her class. She indicated she taught knowledge every Sunday. I am sure some teachers do teach knowledge effectively, and some Christians have a serious knowledge of the Bible. But when most Sunday School teachers say they teach knowledge in every lesson, they do not mean systematic knowledge. Teaching with a knowledge aim means striving for mastery of *systematic* knowledge. When most teachers say they teach knowledge, they do not mean teaching in such a way that the members learn this knowledge at the depth level that I mean.

Overwhelming evidence indicates that even those of us who attend Sunday School have little knowledge of the Bible. This may not be the most serious problem we face as Christians. But it is a tragic problem for a people who make the claim of being "a people of the Book."

How can we solve this problem? Two things must happen in the inner being of the person who asks this question seriously.

▲ Individuals must face up to and admit that they have a problem.

▲ Individuals must make an inner commitment that is deep enough to lead them to do whatever is needed to seek to solve the problem.

This chapter proposes a possible solution to this problem. I am not sure there is a final and definitive solution. In spite of everything the teacher may do, the learner must be willing to make the effort necessary to do the learning. And, ultimately, it is the learner who must do the learning.

Definition of a Knowledge Aim

A knowledge aim is one in which the teacher seeks to lead the class in a serious, systematic study of a significant portion of Bible material leading to understanding and mastery of that material. Each word or phrase in this definition is vitally important.

Serious

Study with a knowledge aim must be a serious study. That is, it must be a serious study on the part of the learner. It takes effort to learn and if the learner is going to learn he or she must be serious about it. The teacher may share with the class a wealth of knowledge during the class period, but it takes far more than hearing or listening to learn. The learner must be sufficiently serious about learning to make the effort necessary to learn. It is the learner who must do the learning.

Systematic

Study with a knowledge aim must be systematic study. That is, the study done during the lesson period must have a systematic arrangement that is clear to the learner. The lessons may involve a chronological study of a biblical character's life. Or it may be a study of some portion of biblical history. Or it may be a careful study of some doctrine or theological issue. Or it may be a careful study of some book of the Bible. But for the learner to learn it, the material and the study must have some systematic or logical arrangement to it.

In the preceding chapter, I stated that most Sunday School teachers who say they teach knowledge in their classes do not mean by knowledge what I mean when I use the phrase "teaching with a knowledge aim." I hope this part of the definition and the illustrations that will be given later will clarify what I mean by "knowledge" when I refer to teaching with a "knowledge aim." However, teaching knowledge with a logical arrangement does not guarantee that serious learning will take place.

Renowned Bible scholars often come to churches to teach some book of the Bible. They distribute detailed outlines of the book, giving chapter and verse. They present the material with a high level of skill and scholarship. New insights are given. Technical information is shared. Bibles are open. Frequent reference is made to the outline. The people, as a general rule, respond to the teaching with deep appreciation and great joy, inspired by the study. But what would happen if the teacher gave a serious examination of the outline of the book studied? My guess is that most would score poorly. But the professor or the pastor teaching the knowledge might protest, "To teach the people a mastery of the outline was not my aim." That is my point! The teacher never really had a knowledge aim in mind. And the learner never put out the effort necessary to master the knowledge. In our churches we have been conditioned only to listen and to enjoy.

Significant

Study with a knowledge aim must cover a significant portion of the Bible material, a significant person in the Bible, or a significant issue (or topic) related to Bible history. That is, for a lesson to focus on knowledge it must cover more of the Bible than is printed in the quarterly. Generally there is sufficient Bible material in the printed passage for an inspiration aim lesson and sometimes enough for a conduct response aim lesson. But very rarely is there enough Bible material in the printed passage for a knowledge aim lesson.

Understanding

Study with a knowledge aim must lead to an understanding of the material. If the knowledge being learned is to have any value to the learner, then obviously the learner must have an understanding of it. Learners studying some part of Old Testament history must understand how this fits in with and relates to the history immediately preceding it and the history immediately following it. There must also be a clear understanding of the significant factors that are taking place in that period of history. In the limited time the teacher has on Sunday morning for the class period, it will be possible to cover only a limited amount of this knowledge. However, it is expected through the years of a person's life there will be numerous opportunities to cover the same period of history. Each time it is studied with knowledge as an aim, knowledge can be deepened and broadened.

> "A knowledge aim is one in which the teacher seeks to lead the class in a serious, systematic study of a significant portion of Bible material leading to understanding and mastery of that material."

Mastery

Study with a knowledge aim should lead to a mastery of the knowledge which the teacher selects for the class. If there is one word in this definition that should stand out more than any other, it is this word *master*. This has to do with the depth of learning the teacher has in mind with a knowledge aim lesson. In conferences I suggest to teachers whenever they have a knowledge aim lesson, that they should include the word master in their statement of the aim to remind them that mastery of selected knowledge is the purpose of this lesson. That is, the aim should begin, "To seek to lead my class members to master . . . "; then identify the particular knowledge the teacher wants the members to master. In a knowledge aim lesson, regardless of what else the class may learn, if the class members do not master the desired knowledge, the teacher hasn't accomplished his or her aim. What happens may be more needful or more important than learning knowledge (and the teacher should rejoice in this), but the teacher didn't accomplish his or her aim for that lesson. The factors helping the teacher know what facts should be mastered will be discussed later. Here it is sufficient to note that certain facts must be mastered.

Lesson Plan: Knowledge Aim

1. Aim for quarter:
   (3 spaces) All suggested spaces are approximations.
2. Aim for unit:
   (3 spaces):
3. Aim for lesson:
   (3 spaces)
4. Begin with interest:
   (5 spaces)
5. Overview:
   (5 spaces)
6. Organization of material:
   (14 spaces):
7. Summary and review:
   (10 spaces:)
8. Assignment and project:
   (remainder of page)

Lesson Plan for a Knowledge Aim Lesson

Earlier in the book I gave a suggested lesson plan for the teacher to use when teaching a conduct response aim lesson. On the basis of the definition of a knowledge aim given above, it seems to me that the teacher needs to have a completely different lesson plan for a knowledge aim lesson. Therefore I would like to suggest a possible lesson plan for teaching a knowledge aim lesson.

Please read through the lesson plan box on the previous page. Then study the explanation of each division of this lesson plan in the following paragraphs.

Division #1: Aim for Quarter

I strongly encourage the teacher to include the word *master* in all knowledge aims to help keep in focus what the aim is for the quarter, unit, or lesson. For every knowledge aim I use the same pattern, "To seek to lead my class to master . . . "; then I state in general terms the knowledge I want the members to master. Since it is unwieldy to list each item of knowledge you want the class to master for a quarter, a unit, or even a lesson, I generally put "to master the major events" (facts, views, etc.) in the quarter, unit, or lesson. The teacher is the one who selects what knowledge is sufficiently significant for class members to master.

In the preceding chapter I also stated I would indicate what I meant by the word *master*. Every Sunday the teacher gives a lot of information members are not expected to remember. But there is some information the teacher wishes the members would remember. By master I mean more than that. I mean I want the members to learn these facts so well they will not only remember them next Sunday, but I want them to learn at such depth they will remember them next month, next year, and hopefully for life. I will discuss later how that might be approximated.

Division #2: Aim for Unit

The unit aim is the teacher's statement of the knowledge selected for class members to master in a given group of lessons. A unit is determined by the fact that the content of a group of lessons tend to "hang together" around a central theme (such as a period in the ministry of Paul, or a major point in theology, or a period in Bible history). A unit may consist of only one lesson, but usually it consists of two or more lessons.

Division #3: Aim for Lesson

The lesson aim is a statement of the knowledge the teacher desires for the members to master for an individual lesson. (The reader might want to turn to the next chapter to see how each of these steps in the lesson plan are worked out in a sample lesson. However, if you do, be sure to continue reading the explanation for each step in the lesson plan given in this chapter so you will understand what is being done in the sample lesson plan.)

Division #4: Begin With Interest

Whatever the type of lesson the teacher is teaching (inspiration, conduct response, or knowledge), at the beginning of every lesson the teacher should begin with something to "spark" the interest of the class. The very first statement the teacher makes in beginning the lesson should always be carefully planned. This should be as carefully planned as is the most important point the teacher makes in the lesson. The first statement should be designed to grab the attention of each class member and the following statements should be designed to deepen their interest and stimulate their desire to study. This may be a question, an illustration, a brief quote from a recent newspaper, or a cartoon. But the most important thing is to get the class members talking in the general area that will lead into the lesson. The more we get the members talking the more interest we will have—*if* it leads into the lesson!

Division #5: Overview

The overview is a very important part of this lesson plan, particularly with the first lesson of the quarter and the first lesson of each unit. In the first lesson of the quarter the teacher should share with the class the major divisions of the knowledge to be covered in that quarter. The major divisions obviously will correspond with the units that have been determined. This is like putting down tall telephone poles (one for each unit), and during the quarter "stringing the lines" between the poles with knowledge learned. But it is imperative that these telephone poles (major divisions of the content being studied) be very clear in the minds of the learners.

For the first lesson in each unit it is important for the teacher to make clear to the class the major divisions of knowledge to be covered in that unit. These would be shorter telephone poles. The knowledge covered in each lesson would be the lines joining the shorter telephone poles together. For the other lessons (that is, the lessons that are not the first lesson in the quarter or are not the first lesson in a unit) the teacher could use the overview to review the past lesson(s) and to connect the previous lessons with the current lesson.

Division #6: Organization of Material

This section of the lesson plan corresponds with the development of the lesson in a conduct response or inspiration lesson. However, the content that is put in this section and the arrangement of this content is quite different from the content and the arrangement used in the conduct response lesson. So in this part of the lesson plan there are two matters that must be of concern for the teacher—first, the content, and second, the arrangement of the content.

Content. The content obviously would be determined by the material that is covered in the lesson being studied. The teacher needs to be aware that there are some quarters when he cannot use a knowledge aim. This depends on the curriculum. Some lessons are basically designed to teach attitudes. These lessons often skip around and use different books of the Bible. However, most of the time the lessons in a quarter can be designed as knowledge aim lessons. Generally the teacher would need to use what we refer to as "the larger lesson" rather than just the verses printed for each lesson; the latter usually do not cover sufficient Bible material to have a knowledge aim.

Other types of curriculum materials provide a good opportunity to teach with a knowledge aim. Unfortunately, the approach sometimes used in writing these lessons discourages teachers from teaching with a serious knowledge aim in mind. Yet there are many stimulating possibilities for teaching with a knowledge aim if the teacher looks for them. Here are some possible studies:

The Life of the Patriarchs

Early Hebrew History

The Eighth-century Prophets

The Prophecy of Isaiah

The Life and Ministry of Jesus

The Missionary Journeys of Paul

The Development of the Early Church (Acts)

Doctrinal studies are also exciting and helpful. Consider studying the doctrine of the salvation relationship in the four Gospels. The possibilities for content are limitless.

Arrangement. The second matter of importance for the teacher in a knowledge aim lesson is the arrangement of the content for learning. It must be a logical arrangement. In a lesson with a conduct response aim, we said the development of the lesson must not be logical in its arrangement but rather should be psychological in arrangement. Now I am saying that in a lesson with a knowledge aim, the organization of the material must be logical in its arrangement. Also, when the content is arranged logically, the learner is able to understand it more clearly, learn it more easily, and remember it longer.

Division #7: Summary and Review

This is one of the most important parts of the entire lesson plan. This section deals with two parts that fuse into one.

Summary. In the previous section the teacher has shared a great deal of information with the class. The members also have brought out other insights and information through questions they have asked and comments they have made. It is not expected nor is it possible for the members to master all of this information. Therefore it is very important that the teacher lift out and list on the chalkboard the five or six points he feels are important for class members to master from this lesson's study. In this way the teacher summarizes for the class the points he wants the class to master for that week.

Of all the points, information, and insights that have been discussed during the class period, how does the teacher know what to list in this summary? The class members would already know some of the material that has been covered, so the teacher would select certain facts that most of the members do not know as the ones they are to master this week. The teacher would select these facts based on two factors. First, what are the most important facts called for in this lesson in light of the aim for the quarter? Second, what are the items which most of the members do not already know? In a knowledge aim lesson the teacher obviously wants to focus on helping the members to increase their knowledge.

161

The number of points that should be listed in the summary is determined by what the member can (or will) be expected to master during the week in light of work (at home and at business), spending quality time with family, and other concerns. As a general guideline, I suggest five or six points. The teacher will determine the number for the class.

Review. Merely listing the points for summary and writing them on the chalkboard is not all that needs to be done. Remember, for a knowledge aim, *mastery* of knowledge is the sole purpose. Through review it is in this part of the lesson that the process of mastering the knowledge begins. The teacher may pass out paper and ask members to copy the points summarized on the chalkboard, and then give them time to study or memorize the points. After a few minutes, he can ask the class to say those points together with him, the teacher, leading them. This will avoid embarrassing one who makes a mistake. After this is done two or three times, review or study the points some more. Then ask for a volunteer to give the points. Get two or three to do this. After this review the teacher tells the class that to recite these points will be one of the first things he will ask for in next Sunday's lesson.

The mastery of the points in this summary begins in the class period with this review. But it must continue during the rest of the week. Indeed, it must be reviewed each day of the week. This really is not as difficult as it may seem. The list can be reviewed while driving to work, or at a traffic light, or while washing dishes. Indeed it can become fun, a challenge. It needs to be noted that after one has covered several lessons in a knowledge aim quarter, the member needs to review the points to be mastered in previous lessons.

Division #8: Assignment and Project

Assignment. An assignment may be given to an individual or to the class as a whole. An assignment is a task given to deepen knowledge. It may be something as simple as reading the lesson for next Sunday. Or the teacher may ask the class to bring anything they can find about the geography of the land of Palestine. Or the teacher may ask for one member to bring a three-minute report on the beliefs of the Pharisees from a Bible dictionary and another to bring a similar report on the beliefs of the Sadducees. Or the assignment may be a task that is related to the project. If the class is working on a project for the quarter in which they are filling in a map showing the three missionary journeys of Paul, the teacher might make the assignment for each member of the class to locate and write the name of the city on their individual map where Paul was ministering in that day's lesson.

When any assignment is made, the teacher must be sure to call for a report the next Sunday. If the teacher has the habit of making assignments and never calling for a report, she can be assured that most (if not all) in the class will ignore the assignment.

Project. The project is a written learning activity done by each member of the class. The project is of such a nature that it cannot be completed until the knowledge aim series is completed. The project can be suggested by the teacher or it may be proposed by the members as they make plans to focus on a knowledge aim series in their class meeting. The project, as a learning activity, is designed to do three things. First, it helps identify the knowledge to be mastered. Second, it helps deepen the learning. And third, it gives the individual and the class a device to help them remember longer and more systematically what they have studied.

Perhaps the best way to explain this part of the lesson plan is to give possibilities. Of course, the teacher and the class should use their own creativity in devising projects. If the class was studying some aspect of early Hebrew history, the project might be for the class to make a chart giving the kings, the dates they ruled, the location of the major events, characteristics of the religious life of the people, the political situation, the social situation, the economic situation, the major religious influences, and the major teachings for each period of the history. If the class was studying a major doctrine of the church, the project might chart the major differing views concerning the doctrine, the leading proponents of each view, the points supporting each view, and the individual member's own view. If the class was studying the missionary journeys of Paul, the project might consist of a geographical chart giving each location he visited on each of the three journeys, the problems he confronted in each area, the major teaching given in each area, and the results of his visit.

Each class member should do the project in the easiest manner and save or file it for future reference. Or someone might make a chart large enough for all in the classroom to see and fill in each week during the entire study that can serve as a guide for members as they make their own charts. A classroom chart can be saved and used as background material the next time this portion of the Scripture is studied.

13

An Example of a Knowledge Aim Lesson

Aim for the Quarter

Aim for the Unit

Aim for the Lesson

Begin with Interest

Overview

Organizing the Material

Summary and Review

Assignment and Project

Anyone who writes a book on how to teach takes a big risk. I am willing to take that risk because I think I have something significant to say. Anyone who then dares to give an example of how to teach is taking an even larger risk, particularly when the example is on teaching knowledge. But remember, I did not say that most of our class members would *do* this kind of study. I did not say that most of our class members would like it or even try it. But there are those who will do it!

Some of our class members are willing to do this kind of serious study, and they should be given the opportunity to do so. Some churches have used this knowledge aim approach with good results. One church even has a group studying elementary Greek. Some people in our churches yearn for serious Bible study.

Must we always pitch our approach to teaching to the lowest common denominator? Yes, it is true that most church members will not do this type of serious study. Please do not misunderstand me. God calls us to reach the masses, and we must meet their needs. We must meet them where they are. I am just as vigorous about defending this point as I am about the point I am making. But everyone in the church does not have the same level of desire or commitment. And we should not hold back people who are willing to engage in serious study because some—even most—people in the same Sunday School class won't engage in serious study. Have a different class for each group, and let each individual choose which class to attend. I simply am insisting that there needs to be an opportunity for those within the church who are willing to pay the price of doing serious Bible study to have the opportunity to do so.

Now let me finally come to a sample lesson with a knowledge aim. Let's say we are teaching adults thirty to thirty-five years of age.

Aim for the Quarter

The quarterly aim is this: "To seek to lead my class members to master (1) an outline of the life and ministry of Jesus, and (2) a chronology of the major events in His life and ministry."

The teacher will select which events are major. All four Gospels would be included in this study. A knowledge aim series would always (or almost always) last for a period of three months or longer. The teacher, in consultation with class members, should determine when to use the knowledge aim.

Aim for the Unit

The unit aim is this: "To seek to lead my class to master the major events in the pre-Galilean ministry." Again, the teacher would determine what to include in each unit and how many lessons would be in the unit.

Aim for the Lesson

The lesson aim is this: "To seek to lead my class to master the major events surrounding the birth and infancy of Jesus." Once again, the teacher determines what to include in this lesson.

Begin with Interest

For this lesson the teacher might ask, "Sue, approximately how long have you been attending a Sunday School, beginning with your teen years? We don't want to reveal any ages, but think back when you started to Sunday School and just give me an approximate number." (Write figure on chalkboard.) "The rest of you, call out how long you have been coming to Sunday School since you were a teenager." (Write their numbers on chalkboard.) Continue: "During that time, each of you has studied the life of Jesus for at least three months each year. Some years we study the life of Jesus for six months." Using the numbers class members have given, calculate on the chalkboard how many times most class members have studied the life of Jesus. Then continue, "I am sure most or all of us feel that we have a fairly good knowledge of the life of Jesus. Now, I want to ask you a question. How many of you can give me an outline of the life and ministry of Jesus?"

This question will probably be followed by a deafening silence! The teacher can interject into the silence a bit of kidding or humor with the class. My experience has been that humor that grows out of and is related to the learning experience encourages learning by the members. A class that is laughing (related to the learning) is a class that is not only enjoying the lesson but also is learning something.

Teacher: "I don't want you to go into great detail, just give a broad outline." This probably will be followed by a bit of squirming in their seats and some grinning. Without waiting too long the teacher could say, "It doesn't surprise me that you can't give an outline. The fact is, I could not give an outline of the life and ministry of Jesus before I began study for this knowledge aim series of lessons. (At least this would be true for many teachers.) Let me ask, why might it be important for a Christian—for us—to know an outline of the life and ministry of Jesus?" The teacher gives time for the members to think about this and let them respond.

Then the teacher would begin to explain to the class the approach for this quarter (i.e., a serious study of the Bible). This teacher might speak briefly about the prevailing ignorance of the Bible. This helps class members realize that they are not alone in their lack of knowledge, and it may create desire for serious Bible study. The teacher might add humorously, "If we were in public school with our knowledge of the Bible, what grade do you think we would be in?" The teacher might continue, "I am aware that our basic Christian life is not determined by how much Bible knowledge we do or do not have. Also, I am aware that all of us left school a long time ago, and most of us don't want to go back. But also I know how deeply each of you loves the Bible. You are committed to the Bible, and I feel you would really like to have a more serious knowledge of the Bible than you now have. Is that correct?" (Perhaps it would be better to have the discussion in this last paragraph in an earlier class meeting or in an earlier class session.)

Overview

This "demonstration" lesson is the first lesson in the quarter so the overview will give the unit divisions. Also, teaching with a knowledge aim for a quarter means the teacher will have to do some serious study of the Bible as well as have some good resource material.[1] In fact the Bible does not give us an exact chronology of the life and ministry of Jesus. So let me share with

---

1. See Thomas D. Lea and Tom Hudson, *Step by Step Through the New Testament* (Nashville, Convention Press, 1992). The first half of this book deals with Jesus' life and ministry. It may also be used as a text for each class member. Another excellent resource is A. T. Robertson's *A Harmony of the Gospels,* Nashville: The Sunday School Board of the Southern Baptist Convention, 1922). Check with your church library and your local library for additional resources on the life of Christ.

you the outline I like best. These also are the five units for this quarter's study.

Overview for demonstration lesson:

1. Pre-Galilean Ministry
2. Galilean Ministry
3. Journeying to Jerusalem
4. Withdrawal into Perea
5. Trial, Crucifixion, and Resurrection

These divisions also are the "big telephone poles" that need to be driven down. Write these units on the chalkboard and ask the members to memorize them.

The teacher should use two techniques to help class members understand these divisions more clearly. This first technique is *map* study. Using a map large enough for all to see easily, locate Galilee, Samaria, and Judea. Show them where Israel is located in relation to Jordan, Syria, and Egypt. This also helps them relate the Bible to current events.

The second is a brief study of *unit divisions*. The following are examples:

Unit 1.   The Pre-Galilean Ministry: Jesus had a very brief ministry in Judea before going to Galilee. Locate both areas.

Unit 2.   The Galilean Ministry: Jesus spent most of His time and had His major ministry in Galilee.

Unit 3.   Journeying to Jerusalem: The teachings and ministry on His journey from Galilee to Jerusalem.

Unit 4.   Withdrawal into Perea: Locate Perea on the map. The teachings and brief ministry on the other side of the Jordan before His final journey to Jerusalem.

Unit 5.   The Trial, Crucifixion, and Resurrection: The last week of Jesus' life and ministry.

Then, looking at the outline only, the teacher should lead the class in repeating the list together four or five times. Reminding them that it is imperative for them to master this outline, tell them you will give them two to three minutes to memorize this outline. Also tell them after that time you will erase the outline and see who can repeat it to you. This is a different kind of learning for the class. On the one hand, it is so simple; on the other hand, it is demanding and can be embarrassing. It is another place where humor is so helpful. If you can get the members laughing together and having a good time, they will cooperate. If not, you may have a problem.

After the allotted time, the teacher asks for a volunteer to give the outline. After three have responded, the teacher then leads the whole class in saying the outline together.

Organizing the Material

Earlier it was pointed out that this part of the lesson corresponds to the development of the lesson in other lesson plans. The question we must face in this section is, "How should the teacher organize the knowledge for the most effective learning?" Someone has said, "Knowledge that is understood is organized knowledge." This person also said, "Knowledge functions in our minds, not in the form of isolated bits, but as unified patterns or constellations."

Contrary to the approach used with the conduct response aim (which is psychological), here I am emphasizing that the arrangement of this material must be logical. It must be logical as to content and it must be logical as to chronology. Since this is the first lesson of the unit, it is necessary to point out to the class the subdivisions of the unit. Actually there are only three lessons in this first unit. However, note that I have listed four subdivisions, since the first two subdivisions are covered in the first lesson:

Unit I. The Pre-Galilean Ministry

1. The Birth of John the Baptist

2. The Birth, Infancy, and Youth of Jesus

3. The Baptism and Temptation Experience

4. The Early Judean Ministry

I would write this whole unit on the chalkboard; however, since the class has already focused on memorizing the outline for the quarter, I would not in this lesson emphasize memorizing the subdivisions.

I would continue by asking a series of questions, letting class members use their Bibles to find the answers and respond.

1. Where did Mary, the future mother of Jesus, live? Luke 1:26–27 (Nazareth, in Galilee). Locate on a map.

2. Who were the parents of John the Baptist? Luke 1:5–13 (Zacharias and Elizabeth).

3. How were Elizabeth and Mary related? Luke 1:36 (They were cousins). Using a map, point out the distance Mary had to travel to see Elizabeth.

4. Where was John the Baptist born? Luke 1:39–40 (The hill country of Judea, probably in or near Jerusalem since his father was a priest). Locate on a map and show the area where the hill country was in Judea. If time permits and the teacher desires she may call attention to the naming of John the Baptist (Luke 1:59–66) and also note that John grew up in the desert areas where he came from thirty years later (Luke 1:80).

5. Where was Jesus born? Luke 2:1–7 (Bethlehem). Locate on map.

6. How many wise men were there? (I am sure the class will respond, "Three.") Then ask, "Where in the Bible does it mention the number three?" Read Matthew 2:1–12. (The number of wise men is not mentioned. Tradition has settled on three because three gifts were given.)

7. How old was Jesus when the wise men saw him? Matthew 2:10–11. Note, "they came into the house." (Actually we do not know how old Jesus was, but we do know this was not the night of Jesus' birth. Mary, Joseph, and the baby had left the inn and had moved into a house. Unfortunately our Christmas pageants have so conditioned our thinking that invariably we place their visit at Jesus' birth. A little thinking will indicate otherwise. These men were students of the stars. If they saw this unique star for the first time on the night of Jesus' birth, they would have had to come by plane to get there the night of His birth. There would have been more than one miracle that took place that night. No, it would have taken them some time to prepare for the journey. Travel by camels was slow and the distance they traveled would have been lengthy for that time. It could have taken months. In fact Herod had all the male children slain from two years old and under "according to the time which

he had carefully learned of the wise men" to try to make sure the one who was born would be killed.)

8. What is meant by swaddling clothes? (These were strips of cloth about three inches wide that were used to wrap a newborn baby.)

9. What is a manger? (It is a trough in which hay is kept for an animal such as a donkey.)

10. Why was baby Jesus placed in the manger? (It was a common first-century practice that after the father left with the donkey for the day's work, the mother placed her baby in the manger as a crib.)

11. What is the date of the birth of Jesus? (All scholars agree that the commonly accepted date we celebrate as the birth of Jesus is incorrect. First the month of Jesus' birth was not in December because the weather would have been too cool for the shepherds to be out watching the sheep [Luke 2:8–12]. Second, the year generally accepted is 5 or 6 B.C. The arguments and rationale supporting this position are so technical it would not be worthwhile to try to explain them.)

12. Eight days after the birth of Jesus, what event took place? Luke 2:21 (Jesus was circumcised. This was common for all Jewish male infants.)

13. There was another Jewish ritual that Mary and Joseph had to observe forty days after the birth of Jesus. Does anyone know what this was? Luke 2:22–32. (Mary and Joseph, who were still in Bethlehem, brought Jesus with them to Jerusalem to the temple, so they could go through the ritual of purification. In Jewish law there were many things that would make a person ceremonially unclean. One of these was the birth of a child. If the mother bore a male child, she was unclean for seven days plus an additional thirty-three days, and for fourteen days plus an additional sixty-six days if she bore a female child. It was in the temple they heard the affirmation and blessing of Simeon and Anna. Luke 2:25–37.)

14. Read Luke 2:39. Did Mary and Joseph go back to Nazareth after this cleansing ritual? (No. We will seek to bring all of the Gospels into our study to get as complete an account of

the life of Jesus as we can. It is now that the visit of the wise men comes into the picture. Turn to Matthew 2:1–12 and give their chronology. "They came into the house, . . . fell down and worshiped him . . . gave their gifts . . . were warned by God and went home another way.")

15. The wise men went home. Where did Mary and Joseph go? Matthew 2:16. (Because of God's warning to Joseph in a dream, Joseph, Mary, and Jesus left Bethlehem and fled to Egypt [shown on map]. It was then Herod became aware the Magi were not coming back to report to him and he "slew all the male children that were in Bethlehem, and in all the borders thereof, from two years old and under, according to the time which he had carefully learned of the wise men.")

16. How long did they stay in Egypt? Matthew 2:19 (Until after Herod's death, thought to be in the spring of 4 B.C. If Jesus was born in 5 or 6 B.C., then Jesus was about one or two years old when Herod died and they left Egypt.)

17. Where did Joseph, Mary, and Jesus go after they left Egypt? Matthew 2:20–23. (Leaving Egypt, they first came to Judea. But they were afraid of the one who was then ruler over Judea, and being warned by God they continued going north to Nazareth where Mary and Joseph lived before Jesus was born. Locate Egypt, Judea, and Nazareth on the map.)

Summary and Review

In this first lesson of the quarter we have covered a lot of material. We have covered the birth of John the Baptist, the birth of Jesus, the date of His birth, the visit of the wise men, the trip to Egypt, and finally, the trip to Nazareth. However, the one thing I want you to master from today's study is the outline of the major divisions in the life and ministry of Jesus. To aid you in mastering this outline we will review one more time. I will write the five divisions on the chalkboard. Let us repeat them together several times. Be sure you have these written down so you can study them this week because, as I told you earlier in the class, to give this outline will be one of the first things I will ask you to do next Sunday.

Assignment and Project

For the assignment, ask Larry to look up John the Baptist in a Bible dictionary in the church library and see if he can find any information about the early life of John growing up in the deserts, (Luke 1:80), and give a one-minute report next Sunday. Also ask Hazel to give a one-minute report on the Jordan River as it relates to the baptism of Jesus. (If these assignment reports are typed, duplicated, and made into a booklet along with the project suggested below, at the end of the quarter each member will have a valuable source of information about the life and ministry of Jesus.)

For the project the teacher, using legal-size paper, should have prepared the outline of a map showing Galilee, Samaria, Judea, the Jordan River, and the northern part of Egypt. Do not put the names of towns or cities or countries on the map. One of these should be given to each member at the beginning of the first class. It is the task of each member to locate and write in (or print) the name of each town or city, river, mountain, country, and so forth, that is significant in the life and ministry of Jesus. It would be nice if they would write in consecutive numbers where each significant event took place and on another sheet of paper they could list the numbers and write in what the significant event was. Then they could tell what happened, where it happened, and when it happened in the ministry of Jesus. Again, at the end of the quarter they would have a valuable source of information.

14

Factors Related to Teaching Knowledge

The Teacher's Knowledge

The Learner's Knowledge

The Learner's Motivation and Purpose

Two Types of Knowledge
> Knowledge as Facts
> Knowledge as Meaning

Four Levels of Learning
> Awareness
> Recognition
> Memorization
> Understanding

Presenting New Ideas

Using Various Methods

Review
> Definition
> Function of Review
> Opportunities for Review
> Drill

Conclusion

▲ ▲ ▲ ▲ ▲ ▲ ▲ ▲ ▲ ▲ ▲

There are some important factors related to teaching with a knowledge aim that need special, if only brief, attention.

The Teacher's Knowledge

Obviously teachers must have some knowledge of the material to be taught. They also must be willing to engage in some serious study. These two factors may create such a great fear within teachers that they will be unwilling even to try to teach with a knowledge aim. This would be tragic, indeed. While it is true the teacher must have some knowledge to share with the class, it is not expected that the teacher be a world-class scholar. For a special study, the teacher may purchase a commentary that will provide additional help. Again, stress that, if we claim to be "a people of the Book," then we ought to be willing to engage in some serious study of the Bible.

The Learner's Knowledge

The teacher also needs a general idea of what learners already know about the area they will study. This knowledge will vary from class member to class member. On the one hand, the knowledge the teacher is seeking to teach must not be so technical or complex the members become confused and then lose interest. Yet the material should not be so superficial that the study fails to stimulate their thinking. The teacher's challenge is to guide the study between these two extremes—being superficial and being overly complex.

The Learner's Motivation and Purpose

The teacher must motivate class members and help them develop a genuine purpose for their Bible study. Remember, the learner must do the learning. The teacher may be deeply interested in and highly desirous for the class to engage in a serious study of some portion of the Bible. The teacher may use correct techniques and approaches, but unless the members have a desire and are willing to put out the effort necessary to learn, no positive learning will take place.

The Sunday School is not like public schools. Sunday School has no examinations. The learner does not pass from grade to grade or receive a diploma. No class member expects a Sunday

School diploma to help him or her get a better job or make a better living.

What motivational tools encourage us to put out the effort necessary to learn? Certainly making a better life should motivate all Christians to put out the effort necessary to make a serious study of the Bible.

Teachers who decide to teach with a knowledge aim for a quarter (or longer) must be concerned about motivation. What will motivate learners for the quarter as a whole? for each lesson? If the class has never before engaged in a knowledge aim study, two or three weeks before the study begins, the teacher should discuss two questions with the class:

▲ Will study with a knowledge aim help you?

▲ What will knowledge aim study require of the class members and the teacher?

This discussion might be done in a special class meeting or, if attendance is not good at the class meeting, it might be done on Sunday morning. Most Sunday School classes are not accustomed to knowledge aim study. This approach has rarely been used in Sunday School. Class members must understand clearly what is involved in this approach and why it is being used. Otherwise, the experience may be a washout.

Two Types of Knowledge

The teacher will be concerned primarily with two types of knowledge—knowledge as facts and knowledge as meaning. Both of these types of knowledge are important.

Knowledge as Facts

Most of the knowledge in the demonstration lesson was factual, dealing with events surrounding the birth of John the Baptist, the birth of Jesus, and the infancy and youth of Jesus. Another study could survey the Old Testament. In three months the class could study an outline and take a broad sweep of Old Testament history. Or the class could make a study of the eighth-century prophets (Isaiah, Micah, Amos, and Hosea). Our ultimate objective is not learning Bible facts, but these facts are very helpful.

Knowledge as Meaning

A knowledge aim series may have as its objective to learn the meaning of the Book of Job, or the meaning of the Book of Hosea. Or the teacher may lead in a study of the meaning of one or more of the great doctrines of the Christian faith. Or the study may include both types of knowledge. Suppose your class was studying the missionary journeys of Paul. Your major emphasis would be on the places he visited and the events that took place in each place. In addition, however, you would explore other questions: Why did Paul make each journey? Why did he visit these places? What is the significance of the events that took place there?

Four Levels of Learning

What do teachers mean when they say they want a class member to learn something? This seemingly simple question turns out to be complex—too complex to investigate in this book. Every Sunday School teacher, however, needs to be aware that there are different levels of learning. Let me mention *four levels of learning related to knowledge.*

Awareness

At the first level of knowledge a person is aware that sometime in the vague past she has heard of a place, a fact, or a bit of information. For example, someone mentions to her the name of one of the countries in the former USSR. In a musing fashion she says, "I have heard of that place." She remembers it as part of the former Soviet Union, but she has no idea exactly where it is, how large it is, what towns or cities are there, or what it produces. She is only aware that she previously has heard the name of the country.

Recognition

On a slightly higher level than awareness, the individual recognizes the fact, the place, or the bit of information, and it has some significance for him or her. Earlier in the book I mentioned that I had a very limited knowledge of nuclear fission. I know it is related to atoms. I recognize the term when I read it, but that is about the limit of my knowledge of nuclear fission.

Memorization

At this third level of learning, one learns something for the purpose of instant recall; for example, the multiplication tables. For the knowledge aim approach this is one of the levels of learning the teacher needs to seek. Obviously, in every lesson the teacher will share with the class far more knowledge than he will expect the class to memorize. Although the amount of knowledge the members are expected to memorize will be very limited, it is also very important.

Understanding

The fourth level of learning requires that the class understand the meaning of the material. For example, the teacher seeks to lead the class to understand the meaning of the Beatitudes. You may wonder why I emphasize memorization in teaching with a knowledge aim. What I am emphasizing is memorizing points in an outline. Also, much of the knowledge will deal with places and events. However, when the knowledge being taught or studied involves meaning, it is imperative that the learner understand that meaning.

Presenting New Ideas

The teacher who uses a knowledge aim should present new ideas gradually. Presenting new ideas too rapidly often blots out the ideas already presented. Just think about sermons you have heard. If the pastor uses too many different points in the sermon, you forget them. And in Sunday School, it is better to lead the members to master a few ideas rather than expose them to a large number of ideas.

Using Various Methods

Those who teach with a knowledge aim should use a wide variety of methods depending on their teaching aim. The teacher who wants to share with the class some information that is not easily available to them will lecture briefly. To secure involvement, the teacher will ask questions and lead in discussion. To clarify, the teacher will give an example. To make the teaching more personal he may tell a story or give a personal illustration.

To help focus the learning the teacher will use the chalkboard, maps, and other visual aids.

Review

Definition

Review is taking another look at (re-viewing) material previously covered in order to deepen understanding, reveal new meaning, or achieve mastery. The teacher must carefully plan review to be sure that it is interesting and meaningful to class members. Review must involve all the members. Too often the more knowledgeable members dominate, answering all the questions. The class members who most need the review are left out. How can the teacher make the review interesting and meaningful to every class member? The teacher must keep this question in mind as she carefully prepares for the review.

Function of Review

By regularly reviewing previous learning, a teacher can help class members in many ways. Here are six benefits of review in the Sunday School class.

1. *Review helps members organize the material.* If the members are to master the material and make it their permanent possession, they must organize it in their minds so clearly that they can carry it with ease.

2. *Review helps members relate new knowledge to what they already know.* They should relate new knowledge to their background knowledge. For example, if the group is studying the conversion experience, they may be led to see the relationship between a regenerate church membership and the priesthood of believers. Or they may be led to see the relationship between this knowledge and the responsibility of parents to teach children in the home.

3. *Review helps members remember what they have studied.* Repetition is a fundamental principle of learning. The good teacher is aware that exposing the class to information once does not guarantee they will learn it. That is why he provides a review—to help the members fix more firmly in their minds the material they have already studied.

4. *Review helps members learn new material.* If the teacher is leading the class in a study that covers several Sundays, she will want to make sure that the class has mastered the material that has been covered before beginning a study of new material. The old material is the foundation. Once she has laid her foundation, she will bring in her new material and build upon the knowledge her class members have already mastered.

5. *Review helps class members clarify points they have misunderstood.* There may be matters that are not quite clear to some members of the class; other members may have mistaken ideas about certain other points. However, as the teacher leads the class to take another look at the material already studied, he has an opportunity to clear up any mistaken or hazy ideas.

6. *Review helps class members determine how much they have learned.* And it also helps teachers see how much learning has taken place in the class. Of course this procedure gives only a rough evaluation, but it can be a helpful tool for the teacher.

Opportunities for Review

Which are the best times for review? Here is a list of four occasions to help teachers find the best opportunities for review.

1. *Near the opening of the class period.* Never begin a lesson by asking, "What did we study last Sunday?" The teacher should always begin the lesson with something that will get the attention of the class and deepen that attention into interest. Review may come near the beginning, but it should never be the very first thing in the teaching period.

2. *Throughout the lesson.* The teacher may review at various points during the lesson, depending upon the amount and the complexity of the material. The teacher must determine when review is needed.

3. *Near the end of the lesson.* The teacher should review near the end of each lesson. The review will identify aspects of the lesson the teacher wants class members to master.

4. *At the end of each unit and quarter.* The teacher should have a more comprehensive review after covering a relatively large block of content. For example, a comprehensive review is helpful after a unit of study and at the end of each quarter.

Drill

Drill is a repetitive activity designed to insure that the learner is able to make swift and accurate responses. Drill obviously involves memorization, as in memorizing the multiplication tables.

What knowledge needs drill? Only that knowledge for which one desires automatic response. Examples would be major points of a doctrine being studied and major events in a period of Bible history. Since class members don't need to remember everything, the teacher should select only an absolute minimum number of points or facts for drill and mastery. Near the end of the lesson, during the review, the teacher can identify for the class the points or the aspects of the lesson that he expects class members to master.

But unplanned drill will almost certainly be monotonous. Drill should be a group activity. The teacher, as leader, should avoid embarrassing class members. Many short drill periods get better results than a few long periods. Here again, the teacher must plan these drill periods.

Conclusion

Christian living and Christian knowledge are lifelong aims. The teacher must decide when to use a conduct response aim for a quarter (or longer period) and when to use a knowledge aim for a quarter (or longer). Both emphases are valid and necessary. No one ever comes close to exhausting the depths of Christian living or mastering a knowledge of the Bible. Even Mother Teresa, who serves so magnificently ministering to the hurting people of the world, particularly in India, falls short of the life to which God calls all of us. The most renowned biblical scholars and theologians never come close to mastering the depths of Bible knowledge. We all "fall short" and "see through a glass darkly."

Part IV

Helping the Teacher

15. How to Teach Teachers

16. Planning for the Quarter

17. The Importance of the Teacher

18. Some Theological
Aspects of Learning

▲▲▲▲▲▲▲▲▲▲

15

How to Teach Teachers

Practice Under Supervision

An Example of Teacher Training
 The Setting for the Practice Session
 My Approach
 Topic for Analysis and Practice
 Practice

Preparing an Aim for Next Sunday's Lesson
 Using Next Sunday's Lesson
 Group Reports
 The Teacher-Trainer

Most training programs for Sunday School teachers produce few results. Often the pastor or minister of education gathers a few teachers to lead a study on teaching. The minister adopts one of the study course books available and tries to teach the material in the book as effectively as possible. The teacher-trainer insists that the teachers take notes. Participants have good discussion. They ask questions. They relate the teaching to the problems they face as teachers. At the end of the study the minister points out how important it is for the teachers to strive for constant improvement in order to be the best possible teachers. They will be urged and exhorted to put into practice the principles they have studied. The pastor or minister of education comes away with a good feeling about the study because there has been good attendance, good interest, good discussion, and a good response.

Participants often enjoy these training sessions, but what are the results? Teachers who take these courses usually continue planning and teaching their lessons in the same old way. Why? Because the training sessions were all theory. Teachers studied principles that were supposed to improve their teaching, but they received no practical, hands-on guidance. They never applied the principles they were being taught! Teacher-trainers should do more than explain educational principles. They should immediately take next Sunday's lessons and let the teachers *practice* using the principles just taught by seeking to apply them in their preparation of next Sunday's lesson—under the guidance of the teacher-trainer.

Practice Under Supervision

Helping pastors, ministers of education, and others who train teachers learn to use this simple but tremendously important approach could revolutionize the training we do for teachers.

Yet studying a book (even this book!) will not produce these results in teaching. Explaining principles is not enough. Teachers must actually put principles into practice. Can you learn this by reading these pages? That depends on other factors. How much do you already know about the area? What is your reading comprehension? Most teachers confess that they have limited knowledge about teaching. I certainly confess that there is still much I don't know about teaching.

In fact, teaching is difficult and complex. Because it is, good teacher training requires a lot of time. If the pastor or minister of education or other equipper seeking to train the teachers is interested primarily in getting awards for the teachers, then this approach is not for them. Since my retirement, in the church where I am now a member I have taught the principles related to the conduct response lesson for several groups of teachers and prospective teachers using the practice under supervision approach, and it has taken us twelve sessions of one hour and a half each. The other side of the coin is, in order to try to save time, if no practice under supervision is done, little or no learning takes place.

Practice under supervision should focus on the teaching aim. Deciding what type of aim the teacher desires for a given lesson and working out a specific aim for this type of lesson may be the most important thing the teacher does in the total lesson preparation. The other steps in planning the lesson are also important, but unless the teacher decides consciously and carefully what kind of learning aims he or she is seeking for the class, the total learning experience for that session may end in failure.

An Example of Teacher Training

Now let me share with you a procedure I have used in training teachers in many churches. I will use the conduct response aim for this example. I am doing this because I believe the most important thing a teacher does is to seek to secure a conduct response in the lives of the member.

The Setting for the Practice Session

When is the best time to teach the teachers? For prospective teachers, I have done this during the regular Sunday School period (including both the department period and the teaching period). Of course this is not the right hour for those who are already teaching classes. Those already in service often use the regular weekly workers meeting. But these regular meetings aren't really long enough to teach both the principle and do the practice under supervision. It really is better for the principles involved in both the conduct response and the knowledge lessons to be taught at a time of their own choosing. They could then practice the principles under supervision during the weekly workers meeting while they are preparing next Sunday's lesson. Obviously the time of this training session would have to fit the time schedule of the teachers.

My Approach

Let me share a sample approach I have often used in teacher training. I am a great believer in visual aids, so I placed a large chalkboard at the front that was clearly visible to all. Also, I wanted the teachers to take notes so I had them seated at large tables. I turned the tables at an angle so the teachers could sit on both sides of the table, take notes, and still face me. I asked the teachers in the same department to sit around the same table in the practice session, so they would be able to work together using the same lesson.

Before the training session, every teacher must read the lesson for the next Sunday. This should be announced to the teachers ahead of time so they can make this preparation. It is not necessary for the teachers to have actually planned the lesson they will teach, but they do need to be familiar with it to join in the practice of applying the principle that has just been taught.

Because of the busy schedules of many Sunday School teachers, it may be that a department will have only one teacher present. If so, let him or her join a group from a department closest in age to his or her own. If a department has only two present, let them decide whether they want to work together as a group or whether they would prefer to join another group.

However, a group can be too large for this practice session. I prefer a group of four. If there are only three or up to five in a department, that is also acceptable. If there are six, I suggest they consider whether they prefer to make two groups of three. The important factors here are to have a group large enough to have meaningful interaction and small enough so each will have to participate. The temptation for some teachers is not to participate. It is the teachers who do the work in these sessions that do the learning. If a teacher does not join in with the others and do the work, it is doubtful any meaningful learning will take place.

Topic for Analysis and Practice

The topic we will use as the basis for this example is this: "How to work out a specific aim for a conduct response lesson." Assume the teacher-trainer has already completed the study of this principle, the teachers have had their break, and they are now ready for their practice session.

At the beginning of this session the teacher-trainer may want to review a couple of the major points taught in the earlier session to refresh the group's memory and to get the participants back in a working frame of mind. For example, he may review the definitions of the three types of aims (knowledge, inspiration, and conduct response), and also the qualities of a good aim (brief enough to be remembered, clear enough to be written down, and specific enough to be attainable). He can have them repeat the three qualities until they are clearly in mind. The teacher-trainer asks if there are any questions about anything discussed in the previous session. When the group indicates that everything is clear so far, they are ready for practice.

Aims

1. Types of Lesson Aims

   A. Knowledge Aim. The teacher seeks to lead the class in a serious, significant study of a significant portion of Bible material leading to understanding and mastery of that knowledge.
   B. Inspiration Aim. The teacher seeks to lead the class to have a deeper appreciation of some spiritual truth or lead them to accept or deepen some Christian ideal.
   C. Conduct Response Aim. The teacher seeks to lead the class to express in a specific way some Christian action—preferably in the following week.

2. Qualities of a Good Aim

   A. Brief enough to be remembered.
   B. Clear enough to be written down.
   C. Specific enough to be attainable.

Practice

The first thing the teacher-trainer might do to give the teachers some actual practice is to help them complete "An Exercise for the Lesson Aim" found in the appendix. Specific instructions for the teachers and my answers are also in the appendix. After giving out these copies, explain to the teachers they are first to review the qualities of a good aim and also review with care the definitions of each of the three types of aims. The teachers will be a bit apprehensive. They aren't accustomed to this kind of exercise in a church-related study. Explain to them the papers will not be taken up for grading. The use of humor is an excellent way to reduce any anxiety they may have concerning this exercise. So tell them this is one exercise where it is impossible to fail, for two reasons. First, it is perfectly legitimate to cheat and look on the paper of any other person—if the person is willing! The only problem is, the other person may be wrong and lead you astray! So, maybe the best thing to do is trust your own judgment. The second reason is even better! Under the column marked "clear," everyone write or print "y" for yes in the block for each aim because each is clear enough to be written down. For doing this, each teacher will pass with a grade of at least 95 percent! *It is important that every block be filled in.* Remember, only the ones who participate really learn. Answer any questions they may have, being sure not to give them the answers on the chart.

Preparing an Aim for Next Sunday's Lesson

As stated earlier in the chapter, this experience of practicing under supervision takes a considerable amount of time. Because this is so very important, let me take just a moment to review the various steps through which the teacher-trainer goes in teaching this to teachers. For the course of study the teacher-trainer will have the five steps in the lesson plan for a conduct response aim lesson and the six steps for a knowledge aim lesson. I always started with the lesson aim for the conduct response lesson and took the next steps in turn. I also found that I could not teach or explain properly the quarterly aim until I had taught all the other steps of the lesson plan. The reader will note that "Planning for the Quarter" is the next chapter. It is usually best to give the teachers a break between the study of the conduct response lesson plan and the knowledge lesson plan.

Up to this point the teacher-trainer has explained as clearly and as fully as possible the part of the lesson plan under consideration. She has divided the teachers into groups of two, three, or four to practice doing what was taught verbally. The teacher-trainer should prepare something unrelated to next Sunday's lesson for them to practice doing (such as the chart with types of aims to be identified. See chart on p. 234.). This will bring up questions and the opportunity for further clarification.

Using Next Sunday's Lesson

The really exciting and important step comes next. Each of the small groups, using their teacher's quarterlies and any other helps, will take the lesson for next Sunday and, working together as a group, write out a conduct response aim, or how to secure purposeful Bible study, or whatever the step is of the lesson plan being studied.

This will take time, but all the time needed must be given. One might say this is the time when the teachers are really learning. Before they were just listening to the trainer talk. Or they were practicing principles on aims or Scripture unrelated to their lesson for Sunday. Now this is real! This makes their work exciting.

But this also makes their work difficult. They are now trying to put into practice an approach they have not been using before. There will be differences among the teachers in the small group on the correct way to do this. The teacher-trainer must check with the different groups to see how each is doing, to answer any questions, and to assist them without doing their work for them.

Group Reports

When most of the groups have finished, the teacher-trainer calls a halt to the work and tells them it is now time for the groups to report on what they have worked out. Each group selects a person from the group to give the report. Because the teachers may feel that giving this report will be embarrassing, the teacher-trainer may have to call on the most secure person in a group to give the first report. Also because of the feeling of possible embarrassment, it is time for the teacher-trainer to inject some humor to relieve the tension. To do this, just before the person giving the first report said anything, I would break in and say something like, "I need to point out to you that the person giving the report for the group is not responsible for what the group worked out!" This has broken the tension and all the groups always cooperated for me.

Before the teacher shares what the group has worked out, the teacher-trainer should ask the teacher for what age group their report is designed (adolescents, youth, adults). Then the teacher reads what the group has worked out. In leading the total group of teachers to evaluate or analyze what this group has worked out, the teacher-trainer should ask the questions that will bring out all the major points in that step of the lesson plan. (See the appendix for guidance in step 1, "Working out a conduct response aim.")

For step 2 of a conduct response lesson, in the next session the teacher-trainer could discuss the various points involved in "Securing Purposeful Bible Study." For the next session the teacher-trainer could call on a teacher to give his or her report on the assignment.

Let me give a suggestion how this might be done. Rather than have the teacher read what he had worked out, the teacher-trainer would say that he and the teacher will act out the plan for securing purposeful Bible study; that is, the teacher-trainer would play the part of one of the class members. The teacher would read or state what the teacher has prepared to say first, then the teacher-trainer would respond as though he were a class member in that age group. The teacher and the teacher-trainer would act out the assignment and in doing so would demonstrate how effective or ineffective the plan was that the teacher had worked out for securing purposeful Bible study. The teacher-trainer would then call on another secure teacher who teaches in another age group, and do the same thing.

After these two sample experiences the other teachers present should be divided into groups of four. The teacher-trainer would explain that one member of the group would play the part of the teacher while the other three would play the part of class members. Let each group select the one who would be first to play the part of teacher. Those playing the parts of class members should be told to be as responsive as they can. This should continue until all four in the group have the opportunity to be the teacher. This way the teachers would see and hopefully learn what was effective and what was not from actual experience.

The Teacher-Trainer

Will practice under supervision produce results in better teaching? Obviously that depends on how clearly and how thoroughly the teacher-trainer has mastered the application of the principles she is seeking to teach. By master I do not mean how fully he or she knows the various points, but how well she is able to help the teachers understand and apply the principles involved in the preparation and teaching of a Sunday School lesson. This is not said to frighten anyone away from being a teacher-trainer. It is simply a statement of fact. A person cannot teach another how to apply a principle in preparing a lesson if that person is not able to do it.

You can see that the teacher-trainer is important. You may be asking yourself, "How can I learn this by reading this book?" How can a pastor, a minister of education, or a layperson master these principles in order to teach and train other teachers? The best way, of course, is to experience practice under supervision by a teacher-trainer who has mastered the application of these principles. In this way the learner absorbs not only the principle but also how it is worked out in practice. But this is not always possible. What can a teacher do in a church where nobody has been exposed to these principles?

My hope is the principles presented in this book are explained clearly and fully enough for a person to be able to study them and apply them. But the teacher would not really know whether the application of the principle was correct. A way to assist with this problem is for the teachers in a department to gather and check on each other as they seek to apply a principle to the preparation of a lesson. But even this does not guarantee that the application would be the best it could be. This indicates the importance of having a teacher-trainer to give this guidance.

16

Planning for the Quarter

Factors Influencing Choice of Lesson Aim
    Knowledge Aim
    Conduct Response Aim
    Inspiration Aim

Nine Steps in Planning the Quarter

An Example of the Nine Steps

Evaluating the Quarter

My wife is a director of an adult department in our church. I am her associate director. I used to travel extensively leading conferences, but now I stay home and sit in on one of the most open, honest, and delightful classes of which I have ever been a part. Our class now has three coteachers. All three are superb in the manner in which they plan for the quarter. At the beginning of each quarter they carefully explain to the class what the focus of our study is for the new quarter. As each subsequent lesson is taught, the teacher clearly relates to what has gone before. I hope all teachers are now following this pattern.

The thesis of this book is this: the teacher should use one and only one of the three types of aims for each lesson. You doubtless remember these three aims: knowledge, inspiration, and conduct response. If you agree with my thesis, you will begin planning for the quarter by asking yourself this question: "Which type of aim will I use for each lesson?" This is a very important question.

Teachers answering this question sometimes choose this scenario. They often adopt a knowledge aim for the first lesson to give the class a knowledge foundation for what will follow. They follow with an inspiration lesson to inspire the class to do something. And finally they use the conduct response lesson to lead the class to do something.

This approach sounds good, but I don't believe it gets good results. In the last chapter it was said when a teacher decided to have a knowledge aim lesson, he should have knowledge as the aim for an entire quarter or longer. So, if the teacher decides to focus on knowledge, the decision is already made as to what type of aim each lesson in the quarter will be. If knowledge is eliminated as the focus for the quarter, this leaves only the inspiration and conduct response aims to be considered. The question then becomes, When should the inspiration aim be used and when should the conduct response aim be used?

In planning for the quarter, the teacher makes these decisions. In making this decision, the teacher should ask two important but relatively easy questions:

▲ Does the class most need knowledge, inspiration, or conduct response?

▲ To which kind of aim does the content of the lessons relate best?

196

If the teacher decides she wants to have a focus on conduct response and inspiration aims for the quarter, then the teacher has some difficult questions to answer. A major question is this: Which lessons will be used with a conduct response aim and which with a inspiration aim? This will be discussed more fully later in this chapter.

There is a third question related to the type of quarterly aim to be used which must be answered as the teacher makes plans for a year: How often should the teacher use a focus on a knowledge aim for the quarter, and how often should he have a focus on inspiration-conduct response for the quarter? This is such a personal decision that I hesitate to make a suggestion. Much depends on the desire and interest of the class members and the teacher. It would seem to me to be wise for the teacher or a class member to bring up this question for discussion during a monthly class meeting and let it be a shared decision. But because I feel so favorable to both of these emphases, I will hazard a suggestion. As a rule of thumb, I like to use a knowledge aim one quarter each year. That leaves the other three quarters for the inspiration or conduct response focus.

Factors Influencing Choice of Lesson Aim

Let me give a few general suggestions the teacher should keep in mind when deciding which of these three types of aim should or should not be used.

Knowledge Aim

A teacher may teach a knowledge aim lesson whenever she feels the needs of the class members call for this type of lesson and the Scripture material for the quarter is usable. However it would be rare for a teacher to teach a knowledge aim lesson unless she had a knowledge aim for the entire quarter. Remember, this does not mean that the teacher will not share some knowledge with the class in every lesson. I am speaking here of teaching a whole lesson with a knowledge aim where mastery of knowledge is the objective. Actually, with a knowledge aim, the teacher only has to make the decision whether the entire quarter (and thus every lesson in the quarter) is to have a knowledge aim. The knowledge aim tends to be all or nothing. That is, the teacher will use a knowledge aim for every lesson in the quarter or will not use the knowledge aim for any lesson in the quarter. Exceptions to this statement are rare.

When the teacher makes the decision about whether every lesson in the quarter is to be a knowledge aim, the whole process of planning for the quarter has been simplified. That is, if the teacher chooses to teach knowledge, then the inspiration aim and conduct response aim have been eliminated from consideration. If the teacher chooses that a quarter will focus on inspiration and conduct response, then knowledge has been eliminated from consideration. So, what seems like a rather complex undertaking turns out to be a rather simple one.

Conduct Response Aim

Assuming the teacher has decided he does not desire to have a knowledge aim for the quarter, this means the teacher has only to decide which lessons will be conduct response lessons and which will be inspiration lessons. From my perspective the teacher must decide first which lessons will be conduct response.

However, there is another very important question: How many conduct response lessons should a teacher have in a quarter? In conferences when I have suggested that it was *not possible or wise for a teacher to have a conduct response lesson every Sunday*, the teachers' first reaction was shock. Then, though they were gracious, invariably they would raise strong objections to my statement. In one conference, the wife of a pastor spoke perhaps what all were feeling. She said, "I would never teach a lesson without seeking a conduct response, as you call it."

I certainly understood how she felt. In fact it is my guess this is what every teacher undertakes to do. That is, in every lesson every teacher seeks to apply the lesson to life. This is what the teacher's quarterly suggests for each lesson. I hope that everyone who reads this book knows that I believe it is highly important that every person, especially every Christian, should seek to apply the teachings of Holy Scriptures to life. And I believe the Sunday School is the agency where this should be done in a special way.

That is not my question. My question is, is it wise for the teacher to seek to apply the lesson to life every Sunday? And my answer is no. Obviously it is necessary for me to defend my position and seek to explain the reasons for my position. I am happy to undertake this because this is one place where I believe I am correct.

First, every teacher I have known has sought to apply the lesson to life. What the typical teacher tends to do is conclude a lesson by urging the class to do something like to go the second mile with Christ this next week (to use one of the aims in the chart). Then the teacher exhorts the class to practice this wherever they go this next week. Then they close with a word of prayer. The likelihood is the class members may resolve they are going to try to go the second mile with Christ this next week, but they never identify where in their world this might be done or what in their world they might do. And it is possible their genuine resolve made in Sunday School will be forgotten by Wednesday morning.

Second, even this is not the biggest problem. Let us suppose the teacher did lead each member to identify specifically one thing he or she can and will do to go the second mile with Christ this next week. Suppose Mary decides to get up every morning fifteen minutes early to begin having a daily period of devotion. After Sunday School, Mary goes to the worship service and the pastor in the sermon urges every Christian to be a witness in the marketplace. Being the conscientious Christian Mary is, she thinks of a friend at work who is not a Christian, and she resolves to witness to this friend this next week. Sunday evening Mary comes back to Discipleship Training where she is urged to do something else to express her commitment to Christ. Then in the message of the evening worship service the pastor exhorts her to do something else. Then on Wednesday night Mary, along with the others, is urged to visit one of the sick sometime this week. We have so many services in the church in which we are exhorted to do something for Christ, that, unfortunately, most of us listen to the exhortation, agree that we ought to do it, but that is where it ends except on rare occasions.

But let us leave out the other services of the church and limit our discussion to the Sunday School. This Sunday the teacher urges the class to go the second mile with Christ and Mary has chosen something specific which she is going to do in her world this next week. The next Sunday the lesson is on loving one's neighbor. Again Mary chooses something specific she will do to express love for her neighbor. Mary recognizes that these are Christian ideals she should seek to make a permanent part of her life. The following Sunday the teacher teaches another ideal and urges the class to express it in daily life. The teacher teaches a different ideal the next Sunday and the next Sunday and the next. Pretty soon Mary, who has seriously been committed to trying to express these ideals in her daily life, cries out silently: "Wait a minute! I've even forgotten what I committed myself to do four Sundays ago! I can't change my life that quickly or that often!" This is true for most of us. We don't change our lives that quickly and that often. And most of us can't remember what we resolved to do four Sundays ago (if we made any resolve).

We come to Sunday School. We join in the discussion. The teacher applies the lesson to life. We agree with what is said. We enjoy the class immensely. Then we go to the worship service and listen again to another exhortation. But it is rare, indeed, that by Wednesday we can even remember what the exhortations were about in Sunday School or in the worship service. At least this is what is true in my life and I don't think I am that much worse than most of you. This explanation has been convincing for me. I hope it has been for you. The teacher really cannot have a conduct response every lesson!

If that is correct, then the question is, How often should the teacher use the conduct response lesson? That can vary. During a quarter it may be three times, two times, or, even one time. For example, one quarter the teacher may have as an aim: "To seek to lead my class members to become more effective witnesses in their marketplaces by building a relationship with and witnessing to a fellow worker." In this quarter there may be some inspirational lessons on Jesus' command to witness and His example as a witness. There may be some lessons on how to build relationships in order to witness. There even may be some knowledge lessons on Scripture to use in witnessing and Scripture to use to meet certain objections. (This would be an exception to the rule of using a knowledge aim for the entire quarter.) But the purpose of all the lessons for the quarter was to seek to lead members to be witnesses in their marketplaces. The teacher would be successful if this happened. The teacher would not be successful if it did not happen, regardless of how much the members enjoyed the lessons! That is, the teacher would not have achieved his or her aim for the quarter.

Now let's come back to our question: How many conduct response aims might a teacher have in a quarter? As a rule of thumb, I say that a teacher should not have a conduct response lesson more often than *once a month,* and that may be too often. What the teacher is seeking to do is to lead a class member to make a desired Christian action to become a *permanent* part of the individual's life, and this takes time.

Inspiration Aim

If the conduct response lesson should be only once a month, that means the teacher will use an inspiration lesson three times a month. This indicates the importance of the inspiration lesson. This does not mean that the inspiration aim is three times more important than the conduct response lesson. The conduct response lesson is the ultimate goal of Christian teaching. I am simply saying the inspiration lesson is a highly important part of the teacher's effort to secure conduct response in the life of each class member.

Nine Steps in Planning the Quarter

These nine steps are listed so the teacher can see clearly the steps that need to be followed in planning for the quarter. They should be followed in this order. Certain words are highlighted because of their importance. An explanation of these steps will follow.

1. Do I desire a knowledge aim for the quarter?

2. Mark all lessons inspiration.

3. Identify which lessons *might* be conduct response.

4. Select the lessons that *will* be conduct response.

5. *Write out* the lesson aim for the conduct response lessons chosen.

6. Select the lessons to be included in each unit.

7. Write out the unit aims. The unit aim for each unit is *word for word* the same as each of the conduct response lesson aims.

8. Write out the quarter aim. The quarter aim is *word for word* the same as all the conduct response aims combined.

9. Identify the *attitude* to be emphasized in each of the inspiration lessons.

Now let me explain these nine steps. Earlier I have indicated various factors that will influence a teacher's choice of when and why to use the knowledge aim, the conduct response aim, and the inspiration aim. Hopefully *I have been convincing in my explanations and arguments because these factors are very important in planning for the quarter.* We are now ready to explain the nine steps through which a teacher must go in planning for the quarter.

Even as I write this I can hear the groans of teachers. My reaction would be the same. But these steps in the main are very simple. Actually steps 4 and 5 *are the only difficult ones in the group. All of the others are a snap.* And when you have completed them, you have done a major part of the preparation of every lesson you will teach this next quarter! Under the leadership of the teacher-trainer and working with other teachers in your department, planning for the quarter will become routine!

Step #1: Choosing an Aim for the Quarter

Ask yourself, "Do I desire a knowledge aim for the entire quarter?" Here the teacher simply makes the choice whether all the lessons for the quarter are to be taught with a knowledge aim. If the answer is yes, the teacher can ignore the other eight steps! This means every lesson in the quarter will have a knowledge aim and the other eight steps can be forgotten! Simple, isn't it? When the teacher chooses to have a knowledge aim for the quarter, all he has to do is write the quarter aims, the unit aims, and the lesson aims, and a significant part of the entire quarter's preparation is completed! On the other hand, if the answer is no, the teacher can completely eliminate the knowledge aim from consideration for the rest of the quarter and be concerned only with inspiration and conduct response aims.

Step #2: Mark All the Lessons Inspiration

Assuming the teacher in step 1 has said, "I do not want to have knowledge as my aim for this quarter," this means the teacher will be concerned *only* with inspiration and conduct response for the other eight steps. Earlier I said every lesson may have an inspiration aim. Therefore in step 2, the teacher will mark all the lessons inspiration. I suggest that you take a sheet of paper and write the numbers 1 through 13 (the number of lessons in the quarter) on the left hand margin from top to bottom. Then by each number, write an "I" for "inspiration" by each number.

Step #3: Identify Which Lessons Might Be Conduct Response

Almost every lesson can be a conduct response lesson. As I write this, next Sunday is Easter. Naturally we are studying the account of Christ's resurrection. This lesson might be a conduct response aim. It could be made an evangelistic emphasis such as to witness to an unsaved neighbor (although the resurrection itself does not have that emphasis). In this step the teacher is concerned only with which lessons *might* be conduct response. Don't waste any time worrying over this point. If there is any possibility that it could be conduct response, go ahead and mark it "CR." (Find the lesson in your list of one through thirteen and mark the "CR" on your sheet of paper. This would mean that this lesson would be marked with both an "I" and a "CR" beside it.) See the table on page 209.

Step #4: Select the Lessons that *Will* Be Conduct Response

After the teacher has read over the titles of the lessons and the Scripture passages related to them and thus has become familiar with the lessons, she can complete the first three steps in about three minutes. In step 3 I told the teachers not to worry about whether or not they marked a lesson conduct response. If there is the slightest possibility it would be conduct response, mark it "CR." But in step 4 the teacher needs to begin to worry. If the teacher can have no more than three conduct responses in the quarter, then it becomes a matter of prime importance which of these lessons will be conduct response!

Obviously this planning for the quarter needs to be done before the quarter begins. This, in turn, means the teacher will need some lesson help that will give at least the titles of the lessons and the location of the Scripture passages that will be used with each lesson. To get this planning for the quarter completed, teachers will need to begin their planning at least two weeks before the current quarter is over.

In a given quarter, how does the teacher decide which lessons will be the conduct response lessons and which will be the inspiration lessons? First, the teacher must look through the titles and the Scripture passages of the lessons for the coming quarter and identify those lessons which can be conduct response (done in step 3). Second, review the lessons that could be conduct response. (In step 3, the teacher finds several lessons that really do not make good conduct response aims. These lessons would make much better inspiration lessons—to deepen a Christian attitude or a Christian ideal.) Third, since the teacher is limited to having no more than three conduct response lessons in a quarter, he or she would ask: As I know my class members, which three lessons in this quarter deal with the area(s) where I and my members most need growth in our Christian lives?

A fourth factor needs to be mentioned. If at all possible, the conduct response aim should *never* be the first lesson in a unit. The ideal for a unit, if possible, is to have two inspiration lessons dealing with attitudes that hopefully lead up to and lay a foundation for the conduct response lesson which follows as the third lesson. The fourth lesson in the unit is an inspiration lesson which serves as a follow-up to the conduct response lesson. (The unit is discussed more fully on pages 206–207.) With these four factors clearly in mind the teacher is now ready to identify and select the lessons that *will* be conduct response.

When the teacher has selected the lessons that will be conduct response, the teacher can erase the I (inspiration) and mark these CR (conduct response). (See the table on page 210.)

Step #5: Write Lesson Aim for Conduct Response Lessons

Write out the lesson aim for the conduct response lessons you have chosen. To write out the conduct response aim (not just have it in your mind) is the most difficult but the most necessary step for the teacher in the whole process. Therefore *it is suggested* that the teacher check very carefully the material on working out a conduct response aim.[1] But for the entire quarter, the teacher has only three conduct response aims to write out at this point.

However, even the material given there will not be sufficient. When I was teaching this to seminary students, I found they really did not understand fully how to work out a conduct response aim for a given lesson until we came near the end of the semester and were talking about planning for the quarter. Perhaps it is the same with you.

The teacher must view the conduct response aim as a growth step for each class member. For those in the class who are unsaved, there will be lessons where the conduct response aim is to lead the unsaved person to accept Christ as Savior and Lord. It seems to me, however, that the evangelization of this person could best be done outside of class in a one-to-one relationship.

---

1. See page 211.

If the conduct response aim is to be a growth step for each member of the class, this means the teacher will need to have a different conduct response aim for nearly every member of the class since different members will have different levels of spiritual development as well as different needs. This also means that as the teacher writes out the conduct response aim he will not have just one conduct response which all the members are to do, but will have several options that will enable each member to express in a concrete and specific way the Christian response in his or her life or marketplace.

However, this raises a problem. One of the qualities of a good aim is that it must be brief enough to be remembered. How can the teacher remember the aim if he has a different response for each member of the class? There is a simple way to eliminate this problem. In writing the aim the teacher will place the word "or" (not "and") after each conduct response listed. For example, if the focus for Sunday's lesson was on the Christian ideal of deepening one's spiritual life and if the teacher chooses to make this a conduct response lesson, the aim may be:

"To seek to lead each member of my class to deepen his (or her) devotional life by:

(1) beginning the practice of daily prayer, or

(2) beginning a time for daily Bible reading and prayer, or

(3) beginning a time for daily family worship, or

(4) beginning the practice of keeping a spiritual journal."

This is a very lengthy aim and violates the quality of brevity to the limit. However, there is one redeeming factor. Each member (if the member chooses to do anything at all) will choose only *one* of these responses (or another one) for his or her response, and the member will be able to remember that one response. The fact is, if a member struggles in the Sunday School class with the question, "Am I really serious about taking a growth step to deepen my spiritual life and if I am, which growth step am I willing to take?" the strong likelihood is he or she will remember it on Monday and through the week. And if there is a follow-up lesson the next Sunday, the member will realize the teacher was serious about the members making a response, and that will deepen each one's commitment.

It is true in studying the various Christian ideals that we all realize we ought to take giant steps in seeking to put these ideals into practice. But the fact is most of us do not take giant steps in changing our lives. Changing our lives is not easy for any of us. As a rule those of us who do try to change and grow in our spiritual lives tend to take small steps, and we stumble and fall, get up, and try again. Making a significant change in the pattern of our lives is not an easy undertaking. Again I say, it cannot be done every Sunday. The only reason we thought it could be done every Sunday was because the teacher made the application, exhorted the members, and thought something was happening. Even if the teacher follows the suggestions made in this book, the teacher will need to build a close, personal relationship with each member of the class so that they can talk intimately with each other to see how things are going. Building personal relations with each member is an essential part of teaching.

Step #6: Select the Lessons for Each Unit

In the approach given in this book the conduct response lesson is the centerpiece for the unit. That is, each unit is built around each conduct response lesson. If the teacher has three conduct response lessons, she will have three units.

In the unit the inspiration lessons are also directly and intimately related to the conduct response lesson in the following manner. If possible the teacher should seek to have three inspiration lessons built around each conduct response lesson for the unit. Let me suggest what I think is the ideal way to build a unit if the inspiration aims will permit.

Begin the unit with two inspiration lessons. Each inspiration lesson is designed to deepen a Christian attitude. Hopefully the teacher can relate the attitude in the inspiration lesson to the aim of the conduct response lesson in such fashion that the inspiration lessons will help prepare each member of the class to be ready to respond when the conduct response lesson is taught on the third Sunday. The fourth Sunday is an inspiration lesson. Again, hopefully, the attitude can be related to the conduct response so the teacher can use this lesson as a followup lesson to the conduct response lesson to review the response each member hopefully made the past Sunday and to encourage him or her to continue putting it into practice. Since there are thirteen lessons in the quarter, one of the three units (if the teacher selects three) will have five lessons in the unit. This extra lesson will also be used as an inspiration lesson and as a follow-up to the conduct response lesson.

There are two more important points the teacher must keep in mind in selecting which lessons will be included in which units. First, the teacher must never begin a unit with a conduct response lesson. In each unit the teacher will need at least one inspiration lesson, two if possible, and three is not too many. These lessons help the class get ready to be willing to make a specific response when that lesson is taught. The kind of conduct responses of which I speak are not easy to make. Preparation for this kind of response is significant. Second, the teacher should not end a unit with a conduct response lesson if it is possible to avoid it. Again, if the teacher is serious about seeking to make a specific conduct response in the lives of the members, at least one (maybe more) inspiration lesson is needed to serve as a follow-up for the conduct response lesson.

Also, I regret to have to say that with this approach the teacher must ignore the units that are suggested in the teacher's quarterly. The writers do not know what type of aim a teacher may desire to use for a particular lesson. They are writing for classes in thousands of churches. Neither do they know the needs of the members in a specific class. So they divide the units according to the Scripture passages. You as teacher are the one who has to make the units, the central truth, the aims, and everything else be specific for your class.

Step #7: Write Out the Unit Aim

Even in the listing of these steps, I began giving some explanation of this step. I state that the unit aim is *word for word* the same as the conduct response aim. Why are the unit aim and the conduct response aim the same? This is quite evident when you stop and think about it. First, the one thing the teacher wants to happen in the lives of class members during this unit is for them to take a positive growth step in line with the conduct response aim. Second, each of the inspiration lessons either will be a preparation for the conduct response aim or a follow-up to the conduct response aim. Thus everything that is done in each lesson of the unit is seeking this conduct response or growth step in the life of each member. The lessons either prepare for it, call for it, or follow it up. This is what I meant when I said above that the conduct response lesson was the center of the unit.

Step #8: Write Out the Quarter Aim

The quarter aim is *word for word* the same as all the conduct response aims combined. The reason for this is the same as given above. How the quarter aim and the unit aim are to be written out will be illustrated in the next section.

Step #9: Identify the *Attitude* for Emphasis

When the teacher has identified the attitude to be emphasized in each inspiration lesson, all of the aims for the coming quarter will have been worked out! This means if teachers will use these nine steps, they will have a significant portion of their lesson preparation completed for every lesson for an upcoming quarter before the quarter ever begins! I recommend it to the teacher most highly. The aims for the conduct response lessons have already been written down in step five. The aims for the inspiration lessons will simply be: "To seek to lead my class to . . . (here insert a statement of the attitude for each inspiration lesson).

The Random House Dictionary of the English Language defines *attitude* in these words: "manner, disposition, feeling, position, etc., with regard to a person or thing."

The attitudes to be identified relate only to the inspiration lessons. I am aware that a teacher should never make a lesson say what it does not say nor mean what it does not mean. I believe very deeply in this principle. However, I must remind teachers that in identifying attitudes they should keep in mind that, if possible, the attitudes for the first two inspiration lessons should hopefully prepare the way for the third lesson, which is the conduct response lesson. And if possible, the fourth lesson (inspiration) should serve as a follow-up. Unfortunately our curriculum materials do not always make this a possibility. So, teachers, do the best you can in working out the attitudes to be emphasized in the inspiration lessons—still being faithful to the Scriptures.

An Example of the Nine Steps

In this example I will go through the nine steps, stating each step and then giving a sample of how each step might be worked out. Please study the material that follows. I have put steps 2, 3, and 4 across the page to save space. Under step 2, I have marked all the lessons "I" for inspiration. Also under step 2, after I selected the lessons that would be conduct response (step 4), I marked through the "I" for the lessons that would not be inspiration. Under step 3, I have indicated how a teacher might work out step 3 by listing all the lessons that might be conduct response. I have worked out step 4 by eliminating the lessons that will not be conduct response. To make the lessons that will be conduct response stand out, I have indicated in the table on page 210 the ones that were not marked out. I hope all the other steps are self-explanatory. The dates, Scripture, lessons, aims, and so forth, are fictitious.

Step 1: Do I desire a knowledge aim? No.

Step 2: Mark all that might be inspiration aim lessons with "I."

Step 3: Mark all that might be conduct response lessons with CR.

Table 1:

	Might Be Inspiration	Might Be Conduct Response
April 4	I	
April 11	I	CR
April 18	I	CR
April 25	I	CR
May 2	I	
May 9	I	
May 16	I	CR
May 23	I	CR
May 30	I	
June 6	I	CR
June 13	I	CR
June 20	I	CR
June 27	I	

Step 4: Choose which lessons will, in fact, use an inspiration aim and which lessons will use a conduct response aim. Not more than three lessons will be marked CR, and these conduct response lessons obviously will not have an inspiration aim.

(When it is decided in table 2 which lessons *will be* conduct response, the corresponding lessons marked "I" for inspiration will be marked out in table 1; these lessons will be conduct response lessons, not inspiration lessons. Likewise, in table 1 the lessons *not* chosen as conduct response lessons will be marked out; they will be inspiration lessons. This may sound complicated, but it is very simple to do. Of the nine steps used in planning for the quarter, steps 4 and 5 are the only difficult ones.)

Table 2:

	Will Be Inspiration	Will Be Conduct Response
April 4	I	
April 11	I	
April 18		CR
April 25	I	
May 2	I	
May 9	I	
May 16		CR
May 23	I	
May 30	I	
June 6	I	
June 13	I	
June 20		CR
June 27	I	

Step 5: Write CR aims for lessons chosen.

April 18: Lesson Aim: To seek to lead each class member to become more involved in the ministries of our church:

(1) by teaching illiterates how to read, or

(2) by tutoring a culturally deprived child, or

(3) by tutoring a youth who is having difficulty in school, or

(4) by working with the international ministry, or

(5) by working with the "small repairs" ministry, or

(6) by working with exceptional children, or

(7) by teaching in the sewing class for mothers, or

(8) by some other ministry of his or her own choosing.

May 16: Lesson Aim: To seek to lead each member of my class to grow in their spiritual depth:

(1) by beginning a regular time for spiritual devotion, or

(2) by beginning the practice of family worship, or

(3) by beginning the practice of keeping a spiritual journal, or

(4) by lengthening the time he or she spends in spiritual devotion, or

(5) by getting a group together to start a prayer ministry, or

(6) by another action of his or her own choosing.

June 20: Lesson Aim: To seek to lead each member of my class to be a witness in his or her marketplace:

(1) by building a deeper relationship with an unsaved coworker by taking him or her to lunch this week, or

(2) by inviting an unsaved coworker and his or her family for dinner sometime this month, or

(3) by inviting an unsaved coworker to Sunday School and worship next Sunday, or

(4) by staying late to help a coworker who is behind in his or her work, or

(5) by seeking to start a prayer group thirty minutes before work begins one day a week, or

(6) by another action of his or her own choosing.

Step 6: Which lessons will be in what units?

Unit I:	April 4–April 25	Lessons 1–4
Unit II:	May 2–May 30	Lessons 5–9
Unit III:	June 6–June 27	Lessons 10–13

Unit I has two inspiration lessons before the conduct response lesson and one after. Unit II has three inspiration lessons before the conduct response lesson and one after. If the teacher had only two conduct response lessons for the quarter, the unit divisions would be quite different. It is the conduct response aim that determines the unit. The teacher will also note in this particular quarter that the units happened to divide according to the month. This will not always be the case.

Step 7: Write out the unit aims.

Unit I: To seek to lead each class member to become more involved in the ministries of our church:

(1) by teaching illiterates how to read, or

(2) by tutoring a culturally deprived child, or

(3) by tutoring a youth who is having difficulty in school, or

(4) by working with the international ministry, or

(5) by working with the "small repairs" ministry, or

(6) by working with exceptional children, or

(7) by teaching in the sewing class for mothers, or

(8) by some other ministry of his or her own choosing.

Unit II: To seek to lead each member of my class to grow in their spiritual devotion:

(1) by beginning a regular time for spiritual devotion, or

(2) by beginning the practice of family devotions, or

(3) by beginning the practice of keeping a spiritual journal, or

(4) by lengthening the time he or she spends in spiritual devotion, or

(5) by getting a group together to start a prayer ministry, or

(6) by another action of his or her own choosing.

Unit III: To seek to lead each member of my class to be a witness in his or her marketplace this week:

    (1) by building a deeper relationship with an unsaved coworker by taking him or her to lunch this week, or

    (2) by inviting an unsaved coworker and his or her family for dinner sometime this month, or

    (3) by inviting an unsaved coworker to Sunday School and worship this next Sunday, or

    (4) by staying late to help a coworker who is behind in his or her work, or

    (5) by seeking to start a prayer group at work, or

    (6) by another action of his or her own choosing.

Step 8: To seek to lead each member of the class:

(1) to become more involved in the ministries of our church by: (a) teaching illiterates how to read, or (b) tutoring a culturally deprived child, or (c) tutoring a youth who is having difficulty in school, or (d) working with the international ministry, or (e) working with the "small repairs" ministry, or (f) working with exceptional children, or (g) teaching in the sewing class for mothers, or (h) some other ministry of his or her own choosing;

(2) to grow in their spiritual devotion by: (a) beginning a time of spiritual devotion, or (b) beginning the practice of family devotions, or (c) beginning the practice of keeping a spiritual journal, or (d) lengthening the time he or she spends in spiritual devotion, or (e) by getting a group together to start a prayer ministry, or (f) another action of his or her own choosing;

(3) to be a witness in his or her marketplace this week by: (a) building a deeper relationship with a coworker by taking him or her to lunch this week, or (b) inviting an unsaved coworker and his or her family to have dinner sometime this month, or (c) staying late to help a coworker who is behind in his or her work, or (d) seeking to start a prayer group at work, or (f) another action of his or her own choosing.

Step 9: Identify attitudes to be emphasized in inspiration lessons.

Unit I: April 4   Preparatory lesson—ATTITUDE: to deepen conviction that God calls everyone to ministry.

            April 11   Preparatory lesson—ATTITUDE: to deepen conviction that God has gifted each of us for ministry.

            April 18   Conduct response lesson

            April 25   Follow-up lesson—ATTITUDE: To deepen conviction that God holds us accountable for our ministry.

Unit II: May 2   Preparatory lesson—ATTITUDE: In the temptation experience Jesus relied on Scripture to overcome Satan.

            May 9   Preparatory lesson—ATTITUDE: Before choosing the twelve, He spent the night in prayer.

            May 16   Preparatory lesson—ATTITUDE: The practice of spiritual devotion must be genuine and not superficial.

            May 23   Conduct response lesson

            May 30   Follow-up lesson—ATTITUDE: Jesus is our example in genuine spiritual devotion.

Unit III: June 6   Preparatory lesson—ATTITUDE: Jesus' example of witnessing in the marketplace.

            June 13   Preparatory lesson—ATTITUDE: Jesus witnesses in the marketplace to the man by the pool of Bethesda.

            June 20   Conduct response lesson

            June 27   Follow-up lesson—ATTITUDE: Jesus heals the centurion's servant in the marketplace.

The reader will note that I have designed attitudes for the inspiration lessons that would serve as an introduction to and preparation for each of the conduct response lessons. For the lesson that comes after the conduct response lessons, I also have designed an attitude that relates directly to the conduct response aim and thus would give the teacher a chance to follow-up on the emphasis made in the conduct response lesson. This gives the teacher an opportunity to emphasize again the attitude which underlies the conduct response lesson and (certainly without any pressure from the teacher) would give the class members an opportunity to share: (1) whether anyone made a decision to take a growth step after last Sunday's lesson; (2) if so, what difficulties he or she encountered; (3) what success he or she may have had.

Evaluating the Quarter

With this approach to planning for the quarter and with this approach to teaching it becomes possible for the teachers to evaluate the effectiveness of their teaching during the quarter. It will not be the kind of evaluation a school teacher uses in evaluating the knowledge a student has learned. Nor will the teacher's evaluation be completely accurate. But if the teacher has three or fewer conduct responses during the quarter, if there is a close relationship and trust between the teacher and the members, the teacher can have a fair estimate of whether any of the members have made a response in their lives.

If this is the first quarter the teacher uses this approach and the response of the members in taking a growth step is minimal, he or she must not be discouraged! First, the teacher is simply finding out that the members probably have not been taking any growth steps in the past. Second, the teacher must recognize that this approach is something new and sometimes frightening to the members. Third, the teacher must realize that it is difficult for all of us to make changes in our lives that demand we do more than we have been doing. On the positive side, the conduct response lessons give the teacher a basis for evaluation.

With all of this in mind the teacher can look back over the quarter and reflect on each member of the class. No, not everyone in the class made a decision to take three growth steps. The teacher may not be sure what each member of the class did, even the ones who were regular in attendance. She may not have that deep a trust relationship with the members where this kind of personal sharing can take place. Or one or more of the members may be the type of person who does not share such intimate details of their lives. But to the best of the teacher's ability, in reflecting back over the quarter she may say; "No, not everyone responded. I do not know about all of the members, but I know of three who made decisions to get involved in one of the ministries of our church and one who said she was going to try to start a new ministry related to a nearby nursing home. There was one who said he was going to start having a period of daily Bible reading and prayer, and four who said they were going to start daily devotions with the family. One of these said this daily devotion period had already begun to transform the whole attitude of the family! There were three who said they had decided to consciously make their marketplace a place for witness, and one who shared with me she was now witnessing to a fellow worker and asked me to pray with her about this colleague. I am thrilled with these responses and next quarter, I get to do it again!" This is the excitement and fulfillment a teacher ought to experience at the end of every quarter!

17

The Importance
of the Teacher

Teachers Must Examine Their Christian Experience

A Plan for Self-improvement
    Essential Qualities of a Good Teacher
    Self-examination

Checking Myself as a Teacher

This Is My Weakest Point—With God's Help I Will Improve

Using the Chart to Improve

▲ ▲ ▲ ▲ ▲ ▲ ▲ ▲ ▲ ▲ ▲

I have repeated an experiment with groups of Sunday School teachers, and I get almost identical results every time. I ask, "Among all the things you have experienced in Sunday School before you started teaching, what one thing was most important to you?" To help them reflect, I have suggested certain possibilities. "Was it a chorus or song you learned during your preschool years? Was it a piece of equipment with which you played in your early years? Was it a lesson that was taught? Was it a story or illustration that stands out in your mind? In the years before you started teaching, what is it you remember most or think of first?" With some of the questions no hands were raised. With some, one hand or two hands goes up. Finally I ask, "Was it a teacher?" Every time it seems that nearly every hand is raised. I have not made a scientific survey, but my guess is that well over ninety percent voted for the teacher! Think back over your own experience. How would you vote?

If the experiences of these teachers are typical of all those who attend Sunday School, then this fact has tremendous significance for teaching and learning. In considering the teaching-learning process great emphasis is always given to educational principles and teaching techniques. This emphasis is proper. But the experiences of these teachers indicate that the single most important factor influencing learning is the *life and personality of the teacher.* This factor has not been sufficiently emphasized in the past.

We have all heard it said, "What you are speaks so loudly I can't hear what you say." This is doubly true with a Christian teacher. Teachers teach for good or ill largely because of what they are. Their attitude toward God and life, their likes and dislikes, their prejudices, their very habits of speech and manner of dress are as inevitably a part of their teaching as any technical skills or methods.

The teacher is like a stained-glass window. The sunshine of God's truth shines through the teacher's mind, spirit, and life. The light takes on the glow and the color of the teacher, whether it be bright and glowing or dark and gloomy. Perhaps you have had the experience of going from the brilliant sunshine outdoors into some church; the moment you stepped inside you had a feeling of being depressed because it was so gloomy. At another time, you may have gone into a church and, as the sun streamed through the stained-glass windows with its bright and cheerful colors, it seemed as though God was truly present. What made the difference? The sunshine was the same. The difference in the color and appeal within the churches was determined by the stained-glass windows through which God's sunshine passed. The same is true of Christian teachers. God's Word is the same. But there are times when it is not as attractive and appealing as it might be. At other times, it glows with magnetic beauty. The difference may be the teacher through whom the Word of God flows.

Teaching techniques and knowledge of content are of little use unless they are used by a teacher through whose life the truth of God may flow in sincerity and purity. Christian truths are better understood when seen in life. God has revealed Himself in nature. He has revealed Himself still more through the words of the prophets. But when He wanted to reveal Himself and His truth completely and finally to the world, He did so through a person—Jesus, His Son.

What does it mean for a person to be devoted to Christ? What does it mean for a person to live a consecrated life? What does it mean for a person to live a life of faith? It is difficult to get a person to understand these spiritual concepts through the use of words alone. But they can be completely understood when the one who seeks after truth sees them demonstrated in a Christian's life.

In the same manner, lives are impressed and changed far more by truths they see demonstrated than by those they hear spoken. This brings up the matter of learning through identification. We learn best from teachers with whom we tend to identify ourselves. Perhaps then the basic need in our Sunday Schools is for teachers whose life, whose personality, and whose Christian experiences are such as will make the Christian life both desirable and attractive. Thus the place to begin the improvement of our teaching is with our teachers. When our teachers are the kind of teachers whose lives embody the truths they seek to teach, we will not need to have fear for the results.

Teachers Must Examine
Their Christian Experience

Basically, teaching is sharing experience. If this is true, that which teachers should desire most of all to share is Christ. But teachers must have a genuine personal experience with Christ, and they must have genuine experiences with Christ in other realms of life. Teachers must know something of temptation and the power of Christ to help overcome these temptations. Indeed, they must have had Christian experiences in all of the relationships of life, for they can share only those things that they have experienced. If teachers simply are parrots to repeat what is said in the lesson helps and have no experience in their own personal life, Jesus may ask them, "Sayest thou this thing of thyself, or did others tell it thee of me?" (John 18:34, KJV)

Sometimes those who criticize modern Christian education point out that in the early church they did not have a program of Christian education. It may be that we have placed too great an emphasis on some of the externals of our program. We need to be called back to what must be the central emphasis in Christian education. Christians in the early church had an experience to share, and they shared it enthusiastically. This is the very heart of Christian education.

A Plan for Self-improvement

If the life and personality of the teacher are such important factors in influencing the Christian development of those taught, then along with seeking improvement in teaching, teachers should try for self-improvement. Near the close of His public ministry Jesus prayed, "For their sakes I sanctify myself" (John 17:19, NASB). In that hour Jesus was setting Himself apart, He was concentrating upon Himself. Yet this was not at all selfish. It was necessary, for in the final analysis what He had to do for the world depended upon what He did and how He reacted in the situation which He was to face.

Even so, Christian teachers must examine themselves. For the learner's sake, the teacher must sanctify self. The teacher must set self apart. For in the final analysis, much of what the teacher will be able to do for the Christian development of the members will depend upon the teacher—his or her life, personality, and Christian experience.

If our teachers are to improve, they must have a plan for self-improvement. Improvement comes not by accident but by conscious effort. The plan must be carefully worked out, consciously entered into, and systematically followed.

Essential Qualities of a Good Teacher

The first step in devising such a plan would be to lead the teachers to make a list of what they consider to be the essential qualities of a good teacher. In working out this list, teachers should be both idealistic and realistic. The probability is that they will major on generalized qualities. For example, someone will suggest that a good teacher ought to be consecrated. That is true, but consecration is such a broad, general term. How should this consecration be expressed in a specific way?

In listing the qualities of a good teacher, be as practical and specific as possible. The following items might be included by teachers as they make their lists:

1. Be regular in attendance.

2. Be on time.

3. Begin preparation of the lesson at the first of the week.

4. Keep a notebook of information concerning the class members.

5. Visit in the home of each member at least once each month.

6. Attend the weekly workers meeting.

7. Follow a systematic plan of Bible study.

8. Have personal, daily devotions.

9. Follow a definite plan for improving teaching.

10. Have a growing Christian experience.

This list may be expanded by the teachers to include whatever qualities they desire. They would perhaps want to consider certain physical qualities such as sound health, neat appearance, sufficient physical energy, or good posture. Even more important are qualities of personality such as cheerfulness, emotional stability, friendliness, approachability, or sense of humor. Qualities of one's spiritual development are the most important of all, yet they are the most difficult to identify and evaluate. Is my relationship with God in Christ alive and growing? What am I doing to develop my spiritual life? What do I do outside of church to express my Christianity? Do I do more than talk about the evils in my community?

After the teachers have worked out the list of qualities that should be in a good teacher, it should be copied in a form similar to the one shown on page 223. This form should then be presented to them along with a challenge, and they should be led to adopt it as their plan for self-improvement. The teacher is to take this sheet home, and during his or her prayer time, alone with God, rate himself or herself honestly and fairly on these qualities. The rating scale may be on a basis of one to ten, or by excellent, very good, good, weak, or poor. After rating self, the teacher should select the one point where he or she is weakest and work on that particular matter for one month. This is being systematic. Psychologists tell us it is easier to concentrate on one weak point at a time than it is to try to concentrate on many in general.

Self-examination

At the end of the month, the teacher should go to the chosen quiet place and check himself or herself again as to the items on the rating sheet. If the teacher has been working on the weak point of being on time, he looks back over the month and sees whether there has been improvement in this. The teacher perhaps finds that there has been some improvement in this weakest point. If so, then he changes the rating on that point from poor to good and selects the next weakest point as the one to work on for the coming month.

The probable reaction of the teacher to this suggested plan will be something like this: "This is very childish. I know I ought to do better and I'm really going to try to improve, but I don't need any silly little plan to help me." Admittedly, the plan is simple. It was intended to be so. However, the real reason the teacher reacts against this plan is that it pins the teacher down closer than she likes to be pinned down. If the teacher can just make a general resolve to improve, in two or three weeks she will forget about it, and the general resolution will no longer be a bother. But if the teacher works out this self-rating scale and, before God, resolves to improve, that little sheet will be a constant reminder to plague and condemn him or her until improvement is made. We had just as well face the fact that unless we have such a definite systematic plan, the likelihood is that we will not improve at all.

The Master Teacher said, "For their sakes I sanctify myself." For their sakes the Christian teacher must do likewise. There must be a *willingness* to improve on the part of each teacher. We must face this inescapable fact. *The one area—the teacher—that is the most important single influence in the learning process is the one area over which we have complete control.* We cannot control the lessons; we cannot control attendance; we cannot control the weather; but we can control and improve ourselves. The question is, "Are we willing to pay the price?" We must consider the lives of those whom we teach; we must consider the God who saved us; we must consider the God-given task that has been entrusted to our keeping. We may rebel at following a systematic plan for self-improvement, but it will help us. It will bless those whom we teach, and God will smile with favor upon us.

Checking Myself as a Teacher

	Excellent	Very Good	Good	Fair	Poor
Regular in Attendance					
On Time					
Begin Preparation of Lesson the First of the Week					
Pupil Information Notebook					
Visit Each Member Once a Month					
Attend Weekly Workers Meeting					
Follow a Systematic Plan of Bible Study					
Daily Devotions					
Definite Plan for Improving My Teaching					
Growing Christian Experience					

This Is My Weakest Point—
With God's Help I Will Improve

October _____	April _____
November _____	May _____
December _____	June _____
January _____	July _____
February _____	August _____
March _____	September _____

Using the Chart to Improve

1. With the names on your class roll and this chart, go to a quiet place to be alone with God.

2. Read each name and visualize each face.

3. Honestly and objectively go over each qualification and ask yourself, "How do I rate?"

4. Look over the checks that have been put in the column marked "Poor." Consider your weakest point, and resolve with God's help to work on this point throughout the next month.

5. Ask God's help in becoming the kind of teacher your class needs and deserves.

18

Some Theological Aspects of Learning

Soul Competency

The Incarnation

Encounter

Grace

▲ ▲ ▲ ▲ ▲ ▲ ▲ ▲ ▲ ▲ ▲

Churches and the public schools deal with the same individuals, but churches do not have the same educational task as the public schools. Educational psychology and learning theories from secular education can help, but churches cannot rely on these insights alone to understand their teaching-learning task. Christian education has a theological dimension that churches must not overlook. A study of certain theological principles may lead us to a clearer understanding of our educational task and of how we ought to go about it. Also we may be led to see the possibility of a deeper kind of learning which we term Christian learning. We may also discover some paths that we must follow if we are to achieve this kind of learning.

Soul Competency

The doctrine of soul competency means that each individual has both the competency and the right under the leadership of the Holy Spirit to interpret the Scripture. Each individual has not only the right but the responsibility to interpret the Scripture for himself or herself. Christian learning is thus individual and personal. Each individual is responsible before God for the response he or she makes to God. Parents, preachers, and teachers must not usurp or take the place of the individual doing one's own studying, one's own thinking, and one's own learning. Learning is something that cannot be done by proxy. The individual must do his or her own learning or else learning does not take place.

Also implied in soul competency is another principle of learning of real significance. Since each individual under the leadership of the Holy Spirit has the competency to interpret the Scriptures for self, he or she thus has insights which are significant and valuable. Therefore the individual has the responsibility to share his or her insights with all others in the learning group. The individual may have insights that none of the others has but which they need. For this reason each member of the group has the responsibility to be an active participant in and contributor to the discussion out of which learning may take place. The teaching-learning process is not a monologue in which one person does all the talking.

We must remember that God is sovereign. He teaches through whom He will. The person who is formally in charge of the learning group is not the only one who teaches. At any given point in the learning experience the Holy Spirit may choose one of the members to be teacher. The emphasis on participation in the learning group then is not simply an educational technique. Participation, each sharing his or her own insights with the group, is based on the biblical principle that each person has direct access to God and thus has the responsibility to share with others what he or she understands God to be saying to him or her. It is wrong for the learner to remain silent when he or she, as a child of God, may contribute to another who is a brother or sister.

Nor can the learner excuse himself or herself from assuming a responsibility for and contributing to the learning that is done by the group by citing a limited education. No effort is made here to minimize the importance of education. But spiritual insights are not conditioned wholly by the amount of education a person has. Often penetrating and life-changing insights are given by those who have had little or no formal training.

The concept of the church as community needs to be considered at this point to counteract a possible extreme individualism that may be latent in the doctrine of soul competency. It is true that the individual has the right to interpret the Scriptures for self, but the individual has a similar obligation to bring his or her views or conclusions before the church as a fellowship of believers (or before any other group) for their analysis, reaction, and possible correction. God speaks to all members of the Christian community and not just to one person alone. Therefore, it is a spiritual imperative for every individual to submit his or her understanding to other Christians in order to benefit from their insights and understandings. God has often used the group to be teacher to the individual.

However, it must be clearly understood that the individual is not bound by the views of the fellowship. In the final analysis the individual has to make his or her own decision. *Because a person is individually responsible before God, the individual must be free to come to his or her own conclusions.*

The Incarnation

When the infinite God undertook to teach us mortals (that is, to reveal Himself to us), He became incarnate in Jesus Christ. At earlier times and in other ways God sought to reveal Himself, but the highest and most effective means of self-disclosure was in the person of His Son. "God, who at sundry times and in divers manners spake in time past unto the fathers by the prophets, hath in these last days spoken unto us by his Son" (Heb. 1:1–2, KJV). Here is a demonstration of the fact that it is in incarnation a person is best able to understand and appropriate what may be termed abstract truth. In the teaching-learning process truth is best communicated when it is incarnate. This suggests three things.

1. Teachers must incarnate the truth they teach. Teachers do not teach most by what they say or even by what they do, but by what they are.

2. Teachers teach through relationships. Teachers probably teach far more by the relationships they have with the class members (both inside and outside the classroom) than by the words they use in the class session. Learning comes through relationships more than through verbal communication. This does not mean that teachers must not be careful about the words they use when they teach; it means they must be more concerned about the relations they have with the learners. If teachers are seeking to teach the love of God to a child, they must *be* the love of God to the learner. If teachers want to share with an adolescent the fact that God accepts him or her even though he or she is a sinner, teachers must be an expression of God's acceptance to the adolescent when that adolescent has been a sinner. It is through relationships that truth is taught and learned.

3. Truth must become incarnate in the life of the total congregation. This is one of the major weaknesses in the modern church. Too often the life of the congregation does not even remotely resemble what they profess to believe. It is recognized that the congregation is composed of sinners saved by grace, but the life of these saved sinners ought more nearly to approximate the way to which Jesus has called us all. The churches seek to teach verbally that the follower of Christ should lay one's life on the altar of God, that he should offer his life as a living sacrifice, that one should deny self, take up one's cross. However, consider briefly an adult male who has lived his life as an alcoholic. He knows little of the Christian life. But suddenly he has a radical conversion experience. He unites with a church. He attends Sunday School and worship. He listens to this high and holy teaching and preaching. But he sees little incarnation of these biblical truths in the life of the congregation. Basically what he sees in the congregation is a large group of pew sitters. Therefore, by what he sees he comes to feel that these hard sayings of Jesus are ideas to be discussed in Sunday School and worship. And so he settles down with the rest of the congregation, giving intellectual assent to these great truths but not a demonstration of them.

It is quite likely that the most powerful human instrument for teaching in the church is the life lived by the congregation. It may be that one of the major reasons for our failure in teaching is that we are seeking to overcome by verbal teaching the demonstration we give (or fail to give) in our incarnate lives. This is virtually an impossible task. Or, to put the matter positively, it is quite likely that our learners will never learn or even take seriously that which we seek to teach until we begin to demonstrate in incarnate fashion what we now put in words. In the first century there may not have been an overabundance of verbal and formal teaching, but such was not needed. The life lived by the congregation gave an incarnate demonstration of what they believed. This was taught. It was from this that the learners learned.

Encounter

There are different kinds of learning involved in the educational task of the church. They are all important, though not equally important, but they must not be confused with one another. There are certain facts the individual needs to learn. There are certain attitudes the individual needs to develop. There are certain habits the individual needs to form. All of these demand a different approach to learning, but there is still a deeper level of experiential learning which the church seeks. This learning takes place when an individual comes into a personal encounter with the living God. It is true that in this type of learning, facts are learned and attitudes are changed, but something more happens. This is the highest of all learning. It is this type of learning toward which the educational task of the church must ultimately point. It is only in the presence of God that a person truly learns and has his or her life transformed.

This type of learning is difficult to explain and even more difficult to achieve in experience. It must be clearly understood that what happens in this type of learning situation is not simply subjective. It is not merely a psychological phenomenon, though it certainly has its psychological facets. As Christians we live in the faith that there is a reality—God—whom we can and must meet. The deepest and most meaningful learning thus takes place in the presence of God. In the learning situation what we are seeking is a response to God, not simply the learning of information or even beliefs, however biblically related they may be. Information and beliefs are necessary instruments, but the teacher who guides learning must always remember that these are just instruments. It is the open, free response to God we seek.

For this reason the one who is responsible for guiding learning must seek to create a learning situation in which individuals feel free to bring their real selves—not the masks they wear most of the time, but their *real selves* with all their sin, failures, and needs—to the open Book, the Bible, in the class session. As the Bible throws its light upon the matter being considered, as various members share their experiences, their successes and failures, as questions are asked and answered, as problems are raised and solutions sought, it *may be* that in such a situation the individual is led to bare his or her life before God. Here the Holy Spirit, who is the great Teacher, may convict of sin. The individual may come to have a deeper and clearer vision of God and of life. The individual may say: "This is right! I see it now! This is what I must do!" Thus all learning on this level always takes place in the spirit of worship because it takes place in the presence of God.

Therefore, it is not enough for an individual to learn information about religion, valuable as this is. It is not enough for the individual to learn Bible facts, valuable as these are. It is not enough for the individual to engage in a discussion in which ideas are enlarged and horizons expanded, valuable as this is. It is not even enough for the individual to develop certain habits which have religious significance, valuable as they are. In spiritual learning the individual must come to meet God!

Parents must share their knowledge with the child; the Christian teacher must share his or her insights about the Christian faith, but this learning too often tends to be primarily verbal in nature. The individual may live his or her life with certain information mastered, with certain beliefs formulated, and with certain habits expressed, but all this may be external rather than experiential. It is only as the individual comes to meet God for himself or herself that the learning truly becomes internalized.

But to meet God is sometimes a difficult and quite often frightening experience. It is true that we talk quite glibly about entering God's presence. Each time we come into the sanctuary to worship, we rush up to the door of God's presence, saying we shall enter. But most often we simply mill around on the outside, for to meet God in living encounter is an awesome thing. We sinners tend to avoid meeting the holy God. We try to substitute other kinds of learning to avoid real encounter. This is one reason this deeper level of learning so often fails to take place. In spite of all our protestations to the contrary, we *do not* want to meet God. The light of God reveals our sins. The fire of God burns the dross within us. To meet God brings conviction, and conviction may lead to change. And, in the main, we neither want to be convicted nor to be changed. For this reason we tend to cut short the process of learning by substituting the learning of words instead of going the next imperative step and meeting God face to face in living encounter. Spiritual encounter involves meeting *God,* not just learning words about God.

Grace

There is another aspect of this picture that must be understood. It is true that we human beings tend to resist coming into the presence of God. To have the light of God's purity shine upon our wickedness is a deeply disturbing experience. But once we open that door and enter His presence, a most amazing thing happens. We find ourselves bathed in the lavish pool of God's grace. Our sins are revealed. We *are* convicted. We *are* motivated to change. But we *are not* frightened. Sinners though we are, we are accepted as we are. We are overwhelmed by His unsurpassing and matchless grace. Thus, only in the presence of Him whose presence we had feared to enter do we find the peace for which our hearts longed. It is in this presence that we find the meaning, the direction, the motivation, the power for learning— and for living.

Those whom God has gifted and called to this challenging ministry of teaching recognize the joy and opportunity we have. But we also must understand clearly the warning James gives about being a teacher (see Jas. 3:1). We strive to avoid false teaching, but we also must seek to be *effective* teachers. We want to teach Bible knowledge in such a way our members will come to know not only the facts but the meaning of Holy Scripture. We want to deepen the attitudes of our members to such a depth of commitment they will begin to take growth steps in their daily lives as an expression of their conduct response. This calls for us to learn and use those educational principles that will help achieve these goals.

However, important as these are, we are aware that more than this is involved in effective teaching. The life lived by the teacher and the relationship the teacher builds with each member is as important, if not more important, than any educational principle. With this awareness the teacher cries out, "Who is sufficient for these things?" And the teacher becomes even more aware that we all stand in need of God's grace. It is only within the scope of God's amazing grace that all of us must live our lives!

Appendix

Completing "An Exercise for the Lesson Aim"

This exercise is to be used during a teacher training session and completed under the leadership of a teacher-trainer. Duplicate "An Exercise for the Lesson Aim" on the next page for each teacher and follow the instructions below.

1. Tell the teachers to read each aim, and, with the definitions of conduct response, inspiration, and knowledge aims given earlier in this book, decide what type of aim each is. Then in the first column under "Type," the teacher is to write a "CR" if he or she thinks it is a conduct response aim; "I," an inspiration aim; or "K," a knowledge aim.

2. Under the column "Brief," the teacher is to write "Y" (yes) or "N" (no) if he or she feels the aim is or is not brief enough to be remembered. (By writing only the first letter of a word, no one can tell whose paper it is by the handwriting.)

3. The teachers previously completed the "Clear" column with Ys because all aims are obviously clear enough to be written down.

4. Continuing, teachers should find the "Specific" column and mark Y or N in light of the type of aim they indicated in the first column. If teachers compare answers with neighbors and have different answers, do not worry. Both may be correct! (Of course, they may not also.)

An Exercise for the Lesson Aim

TO SEEK TO LEAD MY CLASS MEMBERS . . .	TYPE	BRIEF	CLEAR	SPECIFIC
to live courageously for Christ				
to grow in the knowledge of Christ				
to live the sacrificial Christian life				
to practice the ideal of Christian stewardship				
to dare to go the second mile for Christ				
to obey Christ in all things				
to follow the Sermon on the Mount in daily life				
to help those in need				
to live a more dedicated life this next week				

The teacher-trainer will then tell the teachers in each group to swap their papers with the group farthest from them. Then tell each group again to swap the papers with a different group. Have them swap until no one knows where his or her paper is.

The teacher-trainer then says, "We each have a paper, but hopefully none of us knows whose paper we have. Not knowing that will make it easier to report what is written on the paper we have. Let's take a look at the first aim." The teacher-trainer calls on a confident teacher to respond from his or her paper to the questions which will be asked: "Mary, will you look at the first aim and tell the group what type of aim it is."

(Each of these aims is brief enough to be remembered, so, to make this more brief and easier for the reader, a Y should be under Brief for each of the aims. Since we have already said Ys should complete the Clear column, we really have to be concerned only about Type and Specific.)

Assuming that the paper Mary reads from has an I for inspiration under Type and Y for yes under Specific, is that correct? Yes, it is. But some of the teachers may object and say, "This is a conduct response aim." To keep down a possible argument, the teacher-trainer should ask, "How many have a paper that says this is a conduct response aim?" Generally, about half of the teachers raise their hands.

Remind them of the questions they are to ask about a conduct response aim. The first question is, "What do I want my members to do?" Some may respond, "We want them to live courageously for Christ." Response to the second question, "How can they express it?" may be varied. One of the teachers may say, "There are lots of things they could do." The teacher-trainer should hold his or her "feet to the fire" with the statement, "Such as . . . ?" or "Name one." If a teacher gives a response that is a good possible "growth step" for one or more members to take, the teacher-trainer should ask, "Why was that not stated as one possible response in the aim?" Someone says, "That addition will lengthen the aim"? Then respond: "If the learner is serious about his or her commitment to make this growth step a part of life, surely the learner would remember it."

However, the more likely response to "How can they express it?" will be silence. The teacher-trainer should then suggest that a teacher using the first aim would probably teach an inspiration lesson. This also means that if the teacher under Type puts I for inspiration and under Specific puts Y that is correct because it is sufficiently specific for an inspiration aim, which deals with a general ideal or attitude.

The teacher-trainer follows the above steps for each aim. The following suggestions will help the teacher-trainer and reader with the remaining aims.

▲ The second aim may have more diversity under Type than the first aim. Three different teachers may label it I, CR, or K, respectively. In any case, it is brief enough to be remembered and clear enough to be written down. However, if it was a knowledge aim, the word *master* was not included. Also, it is too general. It would be more fitting to be a quarter's aim rather than a lesson aim. My guess is it would end up being a very general inspiration lesson, but remember, an inspiration aim can be more general than a conduct response.

▲ About the third aim, the teacher-trainer will again ask how many of the papers the teachers have which say the aim is an I, K, or CR. One teacher may say, "It says a conduct response, but it is really an inspiration aim." Teacher-trainer: "I see you have learned something! Why do you say that?" He or she may answer, "It's too general to be a conduct response aim." The teacher-trainer asks, "How many of you agree with what this teacher has said?" Allow time for responses and discussion. Then ask, "Any questions about the fact that this aim is too general for a conduct response aim and will turn out to be an inspiration aim?" Respond to any questions.

▲ Continue: "We have found that it is relatively simple to judge whether an aim is Brief or Clear. But if you want a conduct response aim, it must be stated in a very specific way. Otherwise, no matter what you intend, it will turn out to be an inspiration." In fact, most of our teaching has been just that. Teachers have sought to "make application," but since the lesson aim was general, no specific decisions were made—class members had no conduct response. There are exceptions of course.

This exercise gets to be somewhat "tricky," so the correct answers to the remaining aims will be given. If you put I under Type and Y under Specific, you are correct because as I have said, an inspiration aim can be relatively general. (In the training session, the teacher-trainer should ask if this raises any questions.) If you put CR under Type and N under Specific, you also are correct. However, if you put CR under Type and Y under Specific, you are wrong! Put aside the papers you have and think about what you put on your paper. (The teacher-trainer will write the words in quotation marks on the chalkboard.)

At some point during the training time, the teacher-trainer may add, "One more, very helpful word about distinguishing between an inspiration aim and a conduct response aim: Watch the verbs in your aim! Note the verbs used in this exercise's aims: 'live,' 'grow,' 'practice,' 'dare to go,' 'obey,' 'follow,' 'help'—action and conduct response words. They sound like, 'I am really going to do something this next week in my life and in my world.'

"But what makes it so tricky as you seek to work out an aim is that these are still incomplete. Often the action verb is followed by something too general. The result is only an idea or attitude: "to live courageously for Christ, to dare to go the second mile, to help those in need, to obey Christ in all things."

This is true for lesson aims in curricula materials as well. The teachers will need to be exceedingly careful and watchful as they seek to write out the aims they will use.

An Exercise for the Lesson Aim

TO SEEK TO LEAD MY CLASS MEMBERS . . .	TYPE	BRIEF	CLEAR	SPECIFIC
"to live courageously for Christ"	I CR	Y	Y	<u>Yes</u> No
"to grow in the knowledge of Christ"	I K	Y	Y	<u>Yes</u> No
"to live the sacrificial Christian life"	I CR	Y	Y	<u>Yes</u> No
"to practice the ideal of Christian stewardship"	I CR	Y	Y	<u>Yes</u> No
"to dare to go the second mile for Christ"	I CR	Y	Y	<u>Yes</u> No
"to obey Christ in all things"	I CR	Y	Y	<u>Yes</u> No
"to follow the Sermon on the Mount in daily life"	I CR	Y	Y	<u>Yes</u> No
"to help those in need"	I CR	Y	Y	<u>Yes</u> No
"to live a more dedicated life this next week"	I CR	Y	Y	<u>Yes</u> No